Teaching With Love and Logic
Taking Control of the Classroom

Completely Revised 2nd Edition

Teaching With Love and Logic
Taking Control of the Classroom

Completely Revised 2nd Edition

Jim Fay and Charles Fay, Ph.D.

 Love and Logic

Love and Logic Institute, Inc.
2207 Jackson St
Golden, CO 80401
www.loveandlogic.com
800-338-4065

ISBN# 978-1-942105-23-7

Interior layout & typesetting: Michael C. Snell, Shade of the Cottonwood, L.L.C., Lawrence, KS
Copyedited by Joyce M. Gilmour, Editing TLC, www.editingtlc.com

 Published and printed in the United States of America

Foreword
by Jim Fay

"Jim, will you sign my book? I'm sorry it's so worn out, but I keep going back to it every time a student throws me something new. To tell the truth, it has saved my career… and probably the lives of some of the kids in my classroom."

Over the years I've heard similar statements so many times that I've lost track of the number of times I have joyfully autographed a *Teaching With Love and Logic* book.

Often I have been handed a tattered and dog-eared book with an untold number of tabs sticking out from the pages. Seeing these treasured books warms my heart beyond belief and speaks to the love and acceptance this book has earned.

On the other hand, it's been in circulation for years, causing Charles and me to consider revising it. Each time we mention this to teachers, they tell us that the content is still strong and they still love it.

We have, however, begun to realize that our experience and research on Love and Logic has led us to a far more refined understanding. This has allowed us to provide far simpler and more practical strategies: ones that apply to today's complex and demanding classrooms.

As Love and Logic has evolved over the years, we have also come to realize how helpful stories, examples, and dialogues are for teachers who are faced with ever-increasing demands for their time and energy. As a result, we became motivated to provide a book filled with stories that actually give teachers the words they can use to both prevent and deal with the nagging everyday problems in the classroom.

So… we became determined to write the very best book on managing the evolving demands of classrooms. This book is dedicated to all of the amazing teachers who skillfully serve youth arriving in their rooms with untold levels of societal, familial, emotional, and behavioral baggage. This book is for all of the wonderful educators who create calm and caring classrooms despite the overwhelming needs of their students and today's unrelenting pressure to guarantee high test scores.

If this book isn't the most powerful and practical book you've ever read on the subject, I will gladly buy it back… no questions asked.

Enjoy,

Jim Fay

Foreword
by Dr. Charles Fay

I was raised with Love and Logic. That's right. I often joke, "That's why I became a school psychologist... so I could figure out what happened to me when I was a child."

A large reason I'm so passionate about this approach is the impact it had on my relationship with my mother and father, Shirley and Jim Fay. Instead of endless power struggles, arguing, and stress, we were blessed to spend most of our time enjoying each other. Even as an adult, I adore both of them.

As a young man, I became intrigued with the notion that the grass might be greener on the other side of the fence. I rebelled... by earning a Ph.D. in behavioral psychology. I wasn't just trained in behaviorism, I became a cult member. A strict proponent of operant conditioning, I came to believe that children have but one basic need: stickers, tokens, pizza parties, and other tangible rewards.

As an educator, I soon hit a brick wall. Most of the troubled, streetwise teens I was working with didn't seem to care much about the rewards... or even the consequences I could provide. I was soon humbled enough to ask my father for advice. Like the father of the prodigal son, he embraced me with loving grace.

My return to Love and Logic over two decades ago changed my professional life and my personal one with my three sons. Occasionally, I fall back on the behavioral principles I learned, as they are good tools to have available in the toolbox. Nevertheless, most of the time I find that life can be so much less complicated and more rewarding when the primary focus is on relationships and meeting the deeper underlying needs of those around me. I hope that you, too, find this true.

Teaching can be a joy!

Charles Fay

Dedication

*This book is dedicated to my devoted and always
unconditionally loving mother, Shirley Fay.
You are with the Lord in peace and joy that is beyond
comprehension. Here on earth you are greatly missed.
I love you!*

Table of Contents

CHAPTER ONE

Teaching can be a Joy!

Nothing's Working

Debi walked into the teacher workroom and immediately spotted the younger teacher who'd joined their team in the fall. Lynne had started the year perkier than a toddler with a new puppy. She was the staff member... every school has one... who started the year showing up early for faculty meetings, sharing her dreams of reaching *every* student, and staying late each day to revise her bulletin board. Now she slumped in her chair, depressed, as if her puppy was lost. Debi inquired, "You look like you're having a bad day. What's up?"

"Nothing's working," Lynne lamented. "They don't respect me. They don't seem to care about anything. I don't know if I can do this anymore."

It was clear to Debi that this young teacher was really hurting. Patting her on the back, she empathized, "That sounds so discouraging."

"Yeah," Lynne replied, "I've tried everything, but these kids won't listen to a thing I say. I can't get any teaching done because of their constant interrupting, arguing, complaining, being out of their seats, and refusing to do their assignments."

Perhaps you've met a teacher like Lynne. Maybe you *are* one. If so, there is hope! Many a career has been saved with simple Love and Logic strategies.

Lynne continued to vent: "I thought teaching was going to be fun. I thought I'd be changing lives. I don't even have time to teach with all of this craziness. I haven't had a good day all year… except when Philip was sick and missed school."

Have you ever met a child with great leadership skills… like the kind some folks use to build crime syndicates or terrorist organizations?

This previously perky young teacher finally admitted, "I just don't like him. The others just feed off of his obnoxious behavior."

The sound of Lynne's own words terrified her: "I… don't… like… him." Guilt ran through her blood. It was overwhelming.

Debi had experienced disliking students. She'd also learned that these are the ones we can actually be the most effective with! She reassured, "Sometimes… some kids are really difficult to like. It's natural to feel that way at times. I had a pretty rocky start myself. I believe in you. Would you like to hear what some teachers try?"

Lynne still needed to vent. "But I've tried everything… like ignoring… like threatening to send him to the principal. He's been to in-school detention more times than I'd like to admit. Did I tell you that I threatened to call his mom and he just laughed in my face and told me try it, and that she'd come to school and kick my &%@#$%!?"

Are there students who really talk like that?

Lynne continued to blurt, "I couldn't believe he said that… then I sent him to the principal… that didn't do any good. He just thinks it is fun to go see Dr. Salazar. Honestly, I've tried to be positive. When I took my teaching methods class, I learned about using the colored card system. He got out of his seat, ripped his cards off the wall and threw them in the trash. I tried using rewards… you know those good behavior bucks we give when we catch 'em being good? He just acts out worse."

Do you know any students who don't respond to traditional behavior management systems?

Do you know kids who aren't that thrilled by behavior bucks or pizza parties at the end of the week? Do you ever get tired of having to act like a vending machine?

Lynne went on, "At the university they said there should be a consequence for every misbehavior. Honestly I try, but it just gets insane. When I stop to give a consequence, six other students start bouncing off the walls. Most of the time I feel like I'm playing Whack-A-Mole… besides… most don't even care about the consequences. They're not afraid of anything we can do to them."

Are you also seeing more students who seem immune to consequences?

Are some students desensitized by the hard lives they experience at home? Are others suffering from entitlement, knowing their parents will always bail them out of the consequences of their actions?

Lynne finally broke down in tears. "I really do love the kids. I even love Philip… and I wish I could enjoy them in the classroom. I don't love what I'm doing with them and I don't like the person I'm becoming. I lose my patience and spend way too much time yelling and threatening. I wonder if I really have what it takes to do this job."

Debi encouraged, "I didn't realize you were having so much trouble. Please don't give up. I can tell you are a hard worker and that you love the kids. Does it help… at least a little bit… to know that I struggled, too?"

With a small glint of hope in her eyes, Lynne replied, "Well… I guess. What changed? I mean, it seems as if you like teaching… and the kids behave so well for you. What made the difference?"

"I have a few minutes after school today," Debi offered. "If you're interested, I could share some of the little things that have turned my toughest classes around. If we put our heads together, I bet we can make them work for you also."

There's Hope!

After school that afternoon, the two teachers met to map out a plan for turning around Lynne's unfortunate situation. Close to tears, she needed help badly.

"I'm so sorry you've been having such a hard year," Debi empathized, "but I'm sure you can turn this around. I remember being in the same boat years ago. Fortunately, things started getting way better the day my principal sent me to a Love and Logic conference. I sat through that day hearing one simple and practical technique after another. As the day went on, I realized these techniques weren't gimmicks. They were ways that I could take better care of myself while getting a lot more cooperation from my students. Now I even use some of the stuff on my husband!"

Lynne laughed.

"Toward the end of the conference," Debi continued, "I was ready to use every Love and Logic skill to become a completely transformed teacher. Fortunately, the presenter cautioned us. I still remember his words:

> *'Be kind to yourself by taking it slow. Experiment with one technique at a time rather than making wholesale changes to your approach. And… before implementing each new experiment, talk with your friends about what might go wrong. That way you can plug the holes before your students find them.'*

"I'd never heard anything like it," Debi relayed. "The other experts had basically told us to stop doing what we were doing and start doing their program instead. The Love and Logic presenter encouraged us to keep using the skills we liked and to gradually integrate these new ones into solving the problems we were facing."

"So… it's like a menu?" Lynne inquired.

"Yeah," said Debi. "That's a good way of looking at it. You pick the ones that seem to fit best. Another idea this presenter shared was the fact that today's tough students are not afraid of adults. We can't possibly scare them into learning or behaving. For many, their lives away from school are far scarier than anything we can threaten them with."

Lynne nodded. "That's for sure. Many of my kids have no respect for authority or themselves. And… it's like they don't seem to care what happens to them."

Debi agreed. "Over the years, our society has taken away most of the consequences teachers used in the past. However, the Love and Logic presenter reminded us of something very important:

'One thing that can never be taken away from great teachers is their ability to get students to love them so much that they don't want to disappoint or hassle them. Relationships form the foundation of all effective classroom management, discipline, and instruction.'

Making a Plan

Debi and Lynne spent almost an hour talking about several Love and Logic techniques. By the end of their conversation, a plan was emerging for how to handle Philip when he refused to stop disrupting class. It wasn't a grand and complicated one designed to cure all of Lynne's classroom management woes in a single blow. Instead, it was a simple one, targeting her most pressing need… to show Philip that she could handle his behavior in a caring, yet powerful way. Things in her classroom would definitely look brighter if she could achieve this goal!

As the plan was developing, Debi cautioned, "Remember that plans always fail if our students can find the weaknesses before we do. If we try something new and it fails, our credibility will be damaged all the more."

Lynne agreed. "They will just see us as being weak."

"That's right," Debi nodded. "Before implementing this plan, let's share it with a few friends. We'll see if they can spot any loopholes the students might use to sabotage it. Then we'll go for it only when we're one hundred percent sure of success."

Lynne added, "So my students need to see that I can handle just about anything without breaking a sweat? Then they'll start to respect me?"

"You bet!" Debi agreed. "And being calm and empathetic, makes it tough for them to resist falling in love with you. From Love and Logic I learned that kids of all ages yearn for role models who are both strong and caring. When they find them, they subconsciously identify with them and are more likely to adopt their values."

"It's just like…" Lynne paused, thinking deeply, "…it's just like how I viewed Grandpa Abe. He was really, really strong and very loving at the same time. He could handle us without breaking a sweat, but he was almost always soft-spoken and encouraging. The older I get, the more I see myself becoming like him."

• • • • •

EXPERIMENT ONE:
Build the Relationship

Debi smiled. "You get this! Your Grandpa Abe gave you a wonderful example of how to connect with students. While we're solidifying your plan for handling Philip when he gets out of control, let's run a couple simpler experiments designed to minimize the likelihood that he will get out of control."

"It would be great if I could prevent this," Lynne agreed.

"That's right," continued Debi. "Love and Logic gives strategies for dealing with problems when they get big, but most of the approach is about keeping them from growing in the first place. Here's something you can do tonight. Consider six things about Philip that are positive. These six things should be true and have nothing to do with his school achievement or his behavior."

"I'm not sure I understand," answered Lynne. "And I'm embarrassed to say that I'm not sure I can think of six *positive* things."

Debi answered, "I'm talking about his interests and things he likes to do. For example, what he likes to wear, or a sport he likes, or hobbies, pets, or friends... things like that. Once you come up with six, put each in this format: 'I noticed that you_____. I noticed that.' Here are a couple examples:

> *'I noticed that you're interested in football. I noticed that,'* or
> *'I noticed that you like to draw. I noticed that.'"*

Lynne was a bit confused. "So it's catching him when he does something good and praising him?"

"No," Debi replied. "It's not about praising him for what you want him to do. It's about building a sincere relationship with him where he sees that you notice what he values. The truth of it is that all of us feel more connected and willing to please when we believe others care about what's in our hearts. We all have a

---

We bring the best out of others when we...

- help them feel special.
- focus mostly on what they do well.
- show that we genuinely like and appreciate them.
- have high expectations and hold them accountable.
- love them for who they are... not who we want them to become.

big need to be noticed and valued for who we are. That's why this can be so powerful."

Lynne's eyes lit up. "It's like kids want relationships way more than rewards."

"Yes, yes, yes!" Debi replied. "That's right. Okay... so after you've created your list of six things you are going to notice, share them with him privately during a time when he's not acting out. Share two 'I noticed statements' this week, two the next week, and two the following week. Whatever you do, don't end the statement with 'that's great!' If by chance he wants to talk with you about what you've noticed, listen. If he gets snippy or sarcastic by saying something like, 'So... whatever!' just respond by saying, 'Well... I noticed that' and walk away."

Students want positive relationships way more than they want rewards.

"But, Debi," Lynne began to doubt, "I don't know what good this is really going to do. I mean, how can something that simple actually work with a kid as difficult as Philip?"

Debi smiled. "Well, Lynne, can you spare ten seconds twice a week to find out? I think before long you're going to get a big surprise."

"Is that something I can start tomorrow if I can make that list tonight?"

Debi nodded. "Sure, Lynne. The sooner you start, the better. The faster you get Philip on your side, the sooner his followers will lose their power over you. Didn't you tell me that the class runs better on the days when he's absent?"

The next day, Lynne arrived at school with a tiny bit of hope and some really large doubts. *How could something this simple really work?* Then she thought of her Grandpa Abe... and Mrs. Squire, her seventh grade science teacher. Both of these people made a huge impact on her life. Both made a natural habit of helping others feel special by noticing what they valued in their hearts.

That day she did some rather strange things that truly confused her students. She met each at the door with a smile, a handshake, and a "thanks for coming." Gone was her stern face, reminders about their behavior, and comments about their homework. All was replaced with the hope that maybe... just maybe Debi was right about that Love and Logic stuff.

As Philip passed by, she whispered, "Hey, Philip."

"What?" he snarled.

"I've been noticing that you like to wear basketball shoes."

"So? Nothing wrong with that!"

"You're right, Philip," she said, while turning away to greet his classmates, but added, "Well... I just noticed that."

Philip looked at her as if lobsters were crawling out of her nostrils. Turning to one of his buddies he quipped, "Teacher's gettin' weird, man!"

• • • • •

EXPERIMENT TWO:
Set Limits with a Whisper

By the next day, Lynne was ready with another simple Love and Logic experiment. When Philip started mixing it up with his neighbor, she saw an opportunity to give it a go. Instead of speaking to him from across the room, she gradually wandered his way, teaching along the way. After passing him by, she pulled a surprise U-turn. Coming up from behind, she bent and whispered in his ear, "Philip, could you save that for Mr. Harrison's class?" Without waiting for a reply, she moved away and immediately resumed the lesson.

She wanted to see what he'd do, but she also remembered Debi's caution:

"The longer you stand next to a defiant kid after setting a limit or asking them to do something for you, the less likely they will comply."

LOVE AND LOGIC EXPERIMENT:
Refusing to Work

STUDENT: "I'm not doing this assignment, and you can't make me."

TEACHER (whispering in the student's ear): "Would you try it just for me? Thank you." (Walk away before the student can answer.)

Resisting the urge to look back or demand compliance from Philip, she kept on truckin'. She did, nevertheless, overhear him grumble his signature line, "Teacher's gettin' weird, man."

While he still wasn't doing his math assignment, he wasn't challenging her... or throwing a fit that made it impossible to teach... or getting his buddies to gang up on her.

Maybe, she wondered, *it's okay... at least for now... if he just sits there and draws pictures. It's a better result than what I've been getting by trying to threaten him into learning. Besides, he might grow more willing to do his work once we develop a better relationship.*

She experienced another revelation... that correcting kids where others could overhear might be causing some of her problems. A thought ran through her head: *I guess I can relate. I don't think I'd behave very well if my husband corrected me in front of my friends.*

Handling 'em Without Breaking a Sweat

As you might remember, Debi encouraged Lynne to experiment with some simple, preventative strategies before implementing her plan for handling Philip's major disruptions. This bought her time to present her plan to three other teachers and to have them predict what might go wrong with it. By the end of the week, she'd plugged the potential holes and was ready to meet with her principal, Dr. Salazar, on Monday morning.

"Dr. Salazar," Lynne began, "I hope to handle discipline in my classroom without creating more work for you. I have a plan and I'm hoping you might have a place where I can send a student for a little cool-down time. I don't want you to feel responsible for dealing with him. I don't want him to be a burden for the secretary by having him in the office, but if there was a place where he could just get himself settled down, that would be a big help. Once he's calmer, he can return to class and I'll deal with him later."

With obvious reluctance, Dr. Salazar replied, "I might support that if I know that you are always doing your best to help students be successful *in* your room. I don't feel good about allowing teachers to send kids out of the room as a first line of response to any sort of problem."

Lynne's friends had helped her anticipate his concern. "I agree. That's why I'm working hard on some Love and Logic techniques designed to prevent problems. Some of these involve relationship-building strategies and ways of setting limits with students so they are more likely to be cooperative."

Dr. Salazar seemed interested. "Tell me more."

Lynne continued, "I've realized that sending students down to you for discipline has led them to believe I can't handle them. Now I see I need to be the one who works with my students. It's like a family. They need to see I'm a caring and powerful enough 'parent' to keeps things safe and orderly. Besides, I'm sure you have more important things to do than being responsible for my classroom management."

Dr. Salazar was pleasantly surprised… and a bit stunned. "Well, it sounds like you've been doing a lot of thinking. I'll support that. In fact, if you have any trouble getting Philip… or any other student… to the office for some cool-down time, let the office know. We'll send someone to assist."

Students need to see that we are caring and powerful enough to establish a safe and orderly classroom.

"There is one more thing," Lynne said. "If I need some additional ideas for what to do with Philip or the other students, would you be willing to give me your thoughts?"

"That would be fun!" Dr. Salazar smiled. "I'll be happy to give my two cents' worth."

Ready for Action

Just like the day before, Lynne greeted her students at the door. Everything was the same... except Philip. He wasn't wearing his usual frown. As he passed, she whispered, "I noticed that you like to draw."

He grunted predictably, "So... teach is gettin' weird, man."

In the past, she'd taken this personally. Now she was beginning to wonder if it had little to do with her and much more to do with his need to feel strong and impress his friends. Or... perhaps it had to do with hurts he was having at home. She realized something else: Love and Logic was starting to change the way she thought about students and the challenges they carried into her classroom. While still troubling, Philip's attitude didn't weigh so heavily upon her shoulders.

Lynne began teaching. This was Philip's cue to initiate a rather loud discussion with his four buddies about various topics such as how boring the class was, whose mother was doing what with whom, and how he was more than capable of kicking so-and-so's posterior with his hands and feet tied behind his back.

Lynne continued to teach, but she began to wander toward the chatty quartet. Pulling a U-turn behind Anthony, she whispered in his ear, "Mr. St. John, in room 102, has an extra chair just inside the door to his room. It's for you. He's expecting you. Please come back just as soon as you get yourself back together. Thank you."

Leaning over to Donovan, she whispered, "And you'll be going to room 108. Mrs. Hightower is expecting you. I want you back soon... just as soon as you can get yourself back together."

Part of her Love and Logic plan involved implementing the art and science of divide and conquer. The "art" of working with a group of students feeding off each other involves asking the most compliant members of this group to leave first. Why? Simply because they are more likely to go! The "science" involves the fact that the most challenging students lose much of their power when they no longer have their minions.

Anthony and Donovan, probably surprised, got up and started for the door. This gave her a chance to lean over and whisper to Travis, "And do you need to go, too, or can you get it together here?"

"What I do?" yelled Travis. "I didn't do nothin'. You're always on my case!"

Still whispering, Lynne asked, "Travis, did I ask in a nice way?"

"So?"

"So either you go," Lynne replied softly, "or we go."

Travis was clear about his intentions, "Not doing nothin' and not goin' nowhere. You can't make me!"

Without breaking a sweat, Lynne ripped herself from Travis's glare and announced to the entire class, "Class, line up, please." Turning to Jayla, she asked, "Would you please slowly lead the class to the cafeteria?"

Is a tough student more likely to leave when he or she has an audience… or none? While developing her plan, Lynne quickly realized it was definitely incomplete if she wasn't prepared for "I'm not going! You can't make me!"

Travis wanted to watch his teacher go down in a ball of flames in front of the class. Lynne was ready for this. As she dismissed the class, she calmly turned to him and said, "And you're staying here, right? Thank you."

Quickly turning to Mike, she asked, "Will you go across the hall and ask Ms. Williams if she could come into the hall where she can keep an eye on her room and this room at the same time? Thank you."

Travis was outraged. He was losing control of the situation. Bursting from his chair, he proclaimed, "You can't make me stay! I'm goin', too!"

Lynne turned to Jayla and said, "Change of plans. Let's lead the class down to the main office."

When a defiant student decides to join along, a Love and Logic teacher is more than willing to allow them... and to deliver them to the office.

The Myth of Immediate Consequences

Lynne had always heard that a consequence must be delivered immediately after any sort of rule infraction or defiance. As a result, she once lived in constant fear that a student, like Travis, would do something outrageous... and she'd be left completely lost for a logical and timely consequence.

Immediate consequences are essential when training mice, rats, pigeons, and monkeys. Fortunately, the children in our classrooms have a much greater capacity for abstract thought and long-term memory! Far more important than the amount of time between the infraction and the consequence is ensuring that when students do create problems we always... always... do *something*. As you'll learn in the following chapter, Love and Logic teachers are reluctant to describe the exact consequence in advance. Instead, they simply inform the student:

"Oh... that was a bad decision... I'm going to have to do something about that."

Or...

"This is so sad. I'm busy right now... but I will have to do something about this."

Sometimes, Love and Logic teachers even keep quiet, allowing a student to believe they have gotten away with something in the short term. Then they do *something*.

I (Charles) vividly remember the seventh grader who demonstrated the power of "something." Quite irritated and unprepared to implement anything other than highly punitive and ineffective measures, I turned to the student and said, "I'm going to have to do something about that. We'll visit later."

Much to my surprise, his eyes widened and a look of sincere trepidation washed over his face. Then he replied, "No… don't do *something*."

Threats of specific consequences never impacted this kid whatsoever. A vague promise of doing "something" really got him concerned. Since that event over twenty years ago, we've seen time and time again that "something" seems to be the most dreaded consequence known to child-kind.

An even greater benefit is that saying "something" leaves our options wide open.

From her good friend Debi, Lynne learned she no longer had to live in a constant state of anxiety. She learned she didn't always have to know exactly what to do in each and every situation. She realized that she no longer would feel forced into threatening consequences that she wasn't truly sure she could deliver. She discovered the following:

> ***When you don't know what to do…***
> ***or you are too angry to think straight…***
> ***delay the consequence.***

With this gift, Lynne felt a renewed sense of confidence and calm as she thought about how she might follow up with Travis regarding his outburst. *Now*, she thought, *I can do this on my terms… when I'm ready… after I've had a chance to talk to some of the other staff and come up with a good plan!*

Philip: Her New Buddy

Dr. Salazar was aware that someone might end up in his office that day for some cool-down time. He expected it to be Philip. Much to his surprise, it was Travis.

Problems with immediate consequences

~~If you don't provide an immediate consequence, the child won't learn.~~

This myth has led many parents and educators to...

- feel like they are incompetent because they can't think of consequences while in the "heat of battle."
- react before taking time to anticipate potential problems with the consequences they are providing.
- react before getting essential support from other adults.
- discipline when they are too angry to think.
- work with kids when the kids are too angry to think.
- lose control and do things they wished they hadn't.

The next time a kid does something inappropriate, experiment with saying: "Oh, no. This is sad. I'm going to have to do something about this. We'll talk later."

As Dr. Salazar encouraged Travis into the office, Travis had some choice words for his teacher. To everyone's surprise, Philip came to her defense: "Trav... man... don't be talkin' 'bout Teach. She weird but not that bad."

As the school day ended, Lynne felt as if she'd just won the Super Bowl. Rushing into Debi's room she announced, "You were right."

Debi was confused. "Right about what?"

"About that 'I noticed' thing for building relationships," Lynne answered.

"Oh," Debi replied, "the Love and Logic guys call that the one-sentence intervention... I suppose because it only takes one sentence twice a week."

Lynne smiled. "I only used it for one week with Philip, and now he's standing up for me! I can't believe it. Now he doesn't think I'm *that bad*."

"I'm so happy for you," Debi replied. "I've been surprised many times by how something so simple can make such a big difference."

"I think it's working on me, too. I find myself being a lot less bothered by Philip... even when he's calling me *weird*. Maybe this technique isn't just about getting kids to fall in love with us… but about helping us see the positive in them."

"Could be," Debi agreed.

"And the plan you helped me with worked great. After I took the class back to the room, they all seemed a lot calmer. It was like this one event helped them see that I could handle anything they threw my way."

"I bet they feel safer, too," added Debi. "There are few things more calming to a class than knowing their teacher can maintain caring control of the classroom."

Lynne agreed, "Yeah, I never thought about that. I guess I've learned a lot of things I didn't realize I needed to learn."

"Oh?" asked Debi. "What are you talking about?"

"For one thing, I'm embarrassed to say that my yelling and correcting students from across the room was causing more problems than I could have imagined. I hadn't realized doing so was forcing students into a corner. All they could do to save face was to argue, get defiant, or constantly interrupt my teaching. Now I've discovered that I can prevent most problems without having to stop teaching. There's something else. Now I have some energy left over at the end of the day for myself."

"That's the best part," agreed Debi.

Lynne continued, "I do have another question. Is it okay to use the one-sentence intervention with all of your students?"

"Only if you're the kind of person who doesn't mind fewer battles with students."

Lynne nodded. "I'm that kind of person!"

CHAPTER TWO

Creating a Love and Logic Classroom

Aiden Meets Mr. Harrison

It was not a dark and stormy night, as some chapters start out. It was a bright and brand new school year, and Aiden had managed to reach the eighth grade. He was a big kid with a big attitude who had never felt very capable at school. To make matters more challenging, his brain was swimming in a soup of new and exciting hormones.

Aiden was jazzed about his first hour class: English. Not really. Pulling his pants up to his knees, he hoped to sneak his way in without being noticed. Oh, the horror! There was the teacher, greeting everyone at the door with smiles, handshakes, and high-fives, and saying, "Welcome, guys, thanks for coming."

Aw, man, thought Aiden, *this guy is like all annoying. "Thanks for coming?" What? We gotta be here. What's he so happy about? Probably just like Old Mason from last year... lots of stupid rules and "Sit down, shup up, or go to the office."*

Yanking his hoodie over his head, he made a quick dash for the rear of the room. "Success!" he muttered as he slumped in a desk. "Made it past the creep." Down deep, all he hoped to achieve was to avoid feeling as bad as he'd felt during the past seven years of school.

LOVE AND LOGIC EXPERIMENT:

Having a Rough Morning

STUDENT: (Enters class with a negative look on his face, throws himself down into his chair, and rolls his eyes toward the ceiling.)

TEACHER (whispering with empathy): "Looks like a rough morning. Anyway I can help? Do you need a little time before you start to work?"

How I Run My Love and Logic Classroom

- I will treat you with respect so you will know how to treat me.
- Feel free to do anything that doesn't cause a problem for anyone else.
- If you cause a problem, I will ask you to solve it.
- If you can't solve the problem, or choose not to, I will do something.
- What I do will depend on the special person and the special situation.
- If you feel something is unfair, whisper to me, "I'm not sure that's fair," and we will talk.

Awakened from his protective daydream, he suddenly heard, "Good morning. My name is Mr. Harrison. I hope you enjoy your year with me. We probably need to go over how I run my classroom."

"Yeah… here it comes," Aiden mused sarcastically. "Probably another deal like last year. Lots of stupid rules. Then you get it for makin' what teachers call 'poor choices.' Pathetic. I don't even need to look at the board. Just gonna be a long list of rules. Then a bigger list of consequences so he can threaten us with what's going to happen the first time, second time, and… on… and… on… until we get booted out. Not even listenin'… same old stuff."

Love and Logic isn't the "same old stuff."

I Will Treat You With Respect

Mr. Harrison pointed at a poster titled, "How I Run My Love and Logic Classroom." At the very top it read, "I will treat you with respect so that you will know how to treat me."

A Love and Logic classroom is built on mutual respect and dignity. Since great educators know that students must see… and experience… this, they provide the model. What will have the greatest impact on our youth? Is it what we preach? Or is it what we practice?

The word "mutual" means that great respect and dignity are afforded to students *and* their teachers. In other words, teachers treat students well and set healthy limits over how they, themselves, are treated. Like all effective limits, these involve only what falls completely within the control of the adult. Since we cannot control the behavior of others, we set limits by describing what we're committed to do or allow… our rules for ourselves. While each Love and Logic teacher will provide slightly different limits, these limits are always designed to maintain the dignity of everyone involved.

Mr. Harrison continued, "I find that I do a lot better job of treating students the way they like to be treated when I have some rules for myself. Aiden's eyes involuntarily flitted to the front of the room where he saw a small chart with the heading, "Mr. Harrison's Rules for Himself":

- I listen to one person at a time.
- I listen to students who raise their hands and wait to be called on.
- I argue at 5 p.m. daily and on weekends.
- I provide full credit to papers handed in on time.
- I grade papers that I can read.
- I will always do my best to help you. I will never try to make you.
- I will spend most of my time helping you see what you do well… not what you do poorly.

Students who believe their rights are being violated,
do not respond positively to teachers' requests.

Aiden was confused. *He's talkin' rules for himself?*

Seeming to read his mind, Mr. Harrison continued, "Yes. These are the rules I try to live by. I'm not perfect. If I violate any of them, I'd appreciate it if you would politely point to my list and remind me in the nicest way you know how."

Noah blurted, "Yeah, but how are we supposed to argue with you after school or on the weekend?"

Mr. Harrison smiled, and said, "And who do I listen to?"

Noah's hand shot up.

"Noah," Mr. Harrison asked whimsically, "do you have a question for me?"

"Yeah, but," he proclaimed, "we can't come at five or on the weekends."

With a warm smile, the wise teacher replied, "I know."

> **LOVE AND LOGIC EXPERIMENT:**
> **Gum**
>
> STUDENT: "We get to chew gum in the other classes."
>
> TEACHER (smiling): "Thanks for letting me know... and what's the rule in *this* room?"

Do Anything that Doesn't Cause a Problem

Again, Mr. Harrison pointed to his poster. "In my classroom feel free to do anything you want as long as it doesn't cause a problem for anyone else."

From years of hard knocks of teaching experience, Mr. Harrison learned that *he* needed to be the judge of whether something caused a problem, *rather than* relying on a long list of do's and do-not's posted on the wall. Besides, he'd also discovered that many students can't resist the challenge of finding creative ways to break the rules… so that our consequences no longer fit. Then we find ourselves pulled into endless battles. The more rules we provide, the more power struggles we experience.

How to Treat Students

Give messages of unconditional respect by interacting with kids as we would with well-respected adults. Students should be afforded dignity even in situations of misbehavior.

Be mindful of the role of nonverbal language. Nonverbal aspects of language carry the most meaning. An impatient facial expression is often remembered for a lifetime.

Concentrate on the development of trust. Components of trust when dealing with kids include having no ulterior motives, being consistent, and acknowledging mutual experiences — the same thing that applies to our relationships with adults.

Place emphasis on individual uniqueness rather than on some hierarchy within the class. Most people respond positively to those who treat them as respected individuals.

Give credibility to kids' feelings. Don't discount their emotions by such phrases as "You don't really feel that way, do you?" Of course they do! This is not to say that we must condone all feelings, but to discount them as invalid is to attack the kid's very inner being.

Remember that misbehavior is a mask for pain or insecurity. Most kids misbehave to hurt back or hide weakness. If we can address these issues rather than only the overt behavior, we are further ahead in the long run.

Attempt to understand a student's mind-set and worldview. Be cautious about seeing kids' behavior through only your lens. The key to relationship building is to understand another's point of view.

Make kids' learning tasks manageable and put components of success within their grasp. This may be because of the students' ability or effort, but, nevertheless, make success available to them, regardless of the abilities or efforts of others in the classroom.

Love and Logic classrooms are also devoted to thinking. Who should do the lion's share? Should it be the teachers or the students? If we spend most of our time trying to micromanage them into behaving, will they have the thinking and problem-solving skills to thrive in a complex, often ambiguous world?

Once again, Noah reached for the sky.

"Yes, Noah," Mr. Harrison said, "go ahead with your question."

"Yeah… like we can do *anything?*"

Mr. Harrison nodded, "Sure… as long as I don't believe it causes a problem for anyone else."

"Yeah… but what if it is a problem?" Noah inquired. "What'll happen?"

If You Cause a Problem, I'll Ask You to Solve It

Mr. Harrison replied as he once again pointed to his poster, "As you can see, class, if you cause a problem I will ask you to solve it. I'm here to help, so I may be able to give you some ideas for solving the problem… that is… if you want them."

When our focus is always on creating consequences for students, who is doing most of the thinking and most of the work? We are. There exists a basic rule:

The person who does the most thinking about a problem will learn the most from the problem.

Love and Logic educators are not opposed to providing consequences when necessary, but they tend to err on the side of expecting kids to simply solve the problems they create.

If You Can't Solve the Problem… or Choose Not To… I Will Do Something

For the first time in his school career, Aiden was actually reading ahead. The next point on Mr. Harrison's poster caught his eye: "If you can't solve a problem, or choose not to, I will do something."

To his own amazement, he raised his hand. "Yes?" Mr. Harrison smiled. "I'm sorry I missed you coming in. What's your name?"

"Bob," Aiden answered. "You say you're gonna do something. So what's that?"

"It depends," Mr. Harrison answered. Gesturing toward his poster, he read, "What I do will depend on the special person and the special situation."

Aiden wasn't taking this lying down. "But you have to tell us what you're going to do. Saying you're gonna do something doesn't mean nothing."

What I Do Will Depend on the Special Person and the Special Situation

"I know it probably seems strange. I'm just a different kind of teacher," answered Mr. Harrison. "It means that I will try to find the best solution or best consequence based on what I know about the situation and the problem. This is going to be different in all cases because everyone is different and every situation is different. All people are unique and all problems are unique, so I won't be telling anyone in advance what's going to happen if they can't or won't solve a problem they create. You just need to know that I'm going to do *something*."

> *I can treat everyone with dignity and respect while not enslaving myself to treating everyone the same.*

Some consequences must be set in stone and made aware to all students. These district and schoolwide policies involve drugs, alcohol, weapons, gang-related attire, and other legal/safety issues. Other issues related to day-to-day life with students are more effectively handled when teachers have the freedom to decide which course of action will most effectively meet the unique needs of the student(s) involved.

A teacher from the great State of Texas shared the following excerpt:

"I'd been working extremely hard with a troubled student. His home life was a shambles, he suffered from neurological problems due to fetal alcohol effect, and he was severely depressed. One day he lost it and told me to do something with myself that typically requires more than one person. With a traditional approach, I probably would have been tied to sending the kid to the principal and seeing him get suspended for three days.

"With Love and Logic, I was able to experiment with what I believed would help him more. That was for me to tell him that I still cared for him and to have him spend a week of his free time helping me with some things around the classroom. By the time he was done dusting bookshelves, filing papers, throwing away the dead pens from my desk, and other silly stuff, we had bonded. He and I were the greatest of buddies. What this unique kid needed was to do something positive and to connect with someone."

One of the most powerful aspects of this approach is that it encourages educators to address the problems caused by students, rather than relying on a system… or our administration… to solve these problems. Students develop respect for teachers who care enough about them to deal with the problem directly. Students lack respect for teachers who rely on impersonal systems… or "a trip to the principal" each time a challenge arises. I (Charles) overheard a wonderfully effective teacher addressing a student who'd purposefully damaged her bulletin board:

The student yelled, "Go ahead! Send me to the principal! I don't care."

With warm assertion, her teacher replied, "Oh. You are welcome to spend some time down there to calm down. Then you and I will talk. This is between you and me... not between you and the principal."

This same teacher often joked with her students:

"Kids are always begging to be sent to the principal for a talking to. I don't do that. I'm not that nice. We're a family, and we solve our own problems."

By the way, she worked with very difficult students... and they adored her!

If You Feel Something is Unfair, Whisper to Me

Mr. Harrison continued, "There may be times when you feel something I've done is not fair. As it says on this poster, I want you to let me know. There are several ways students try to do that. Some yell and say, 'That's not fair!' Some come to me and whisper, 'I'm not sure that's fair.' Which style do you think I prefer to listen to?"

Rudy interrupted with a dose of his typical sarcasm, "So I suppose you're going to change what you do if we say that? Are you serious?"

Mr. Harrison acted as if he didn't hear.

"Why aren't you answering my question?" Rudy demanded.

A rather tense silence ensued.

"Because, Rudeeeeeee, he listens when you raise your hand and wait to get called on!" Kendra lectured, kicking the back of Rudy's seat.

Rudy raised his hand.

"Yes, Rudy, what's on your mind?" Mr. Harrison inquired.

"Are you for real?" Rudy questioned.

"You bet!" Mr. Harrison laughed. "If you don't think I'm being fair, you can come to me and let me know by whispering. I'll listen to your opinion at a time when it's convenient for me. If you can present a good case, I may be willing to change my mind about what needs to happen. To be clear, I won't always change my mind. It will all depend on the unique situation and how respectfully you present it. This is my guarantee to you. The legal system often calls this 'due process,' meaning that the accused should always get a chance to tell his or her side of the story."

He then went to his consequence poster and wrote the guarantee in his own handwriting. He signed and dated his statement.

> ### Deal with discipline problems or student complaints on your own terms, so they don't control you.

Hey, thought Aiden, *he might be serious. Maybe this class won't be as bad as I thought. Might be… might not be. Talk's cheap. We'll see.*

Aiden's Problem

It wasn't long before Aiden found himself with a problem. The problem was named Gabriel… or "G" as most folks called him. "G" had been talking trash and disrespecting Aiden since he moved into the neighborhood a year ago. It came to a head in Mr. Harrison's class as "G" stepped over the line by glaring Aiden's way and flashing him some sign language." Jumping out of his chair, Aiden yelled, "You just wrote a check your &$$ can't cover!" To be clear, he wasn't talking about a fraudulent financial transaction. He was indicating, "You just picked a fight that you ain't man enough to win!"

"G" countered by suggesting that Aiden lacked the anatomical features require to make good on his promise.

Fortunately for everyone, this wasn't Mr. Harrison's first rodeo. Quickly moving their way, he calmly replied, "Gabriel, Mrs.

Three Styles of Teaching

Helicopters...

- rescue and rotate their lives around their students.
- think and problem solve for their students.
- feel exhausted and often resentful.
- say, "I'll think through that problem for you."
- send the unstated message: "You are incapable of thinking for yourself and being responsible."

Drill Sergeants...

- bark out orders and tell their students what to choose.
- turn up the volume and threaten.
- feel stressed and frustrated.
- send the unstated message: "You can't think, so I'll do it for you."

Consultants...

- set limits describing what they are going to do or allow.
- enforce these limits with sincere empathy.
- guide students toward making choices and solving problems.
- send the unstated message: "The quality of your life will depend on the quality of your choices. I believe in you."

Wilcox has a seat next-door for you. Come back as soon as you can be here without causing a problem. Aiden, Mr. Ramirez has a place where you can calm down. Come back as soon as you are calm."

Like Vesuvius, Aiden erupted, "You can't tell me what to do!" and stomped out of the building.

Mr. Harrison called Aiden's mother and informed her about the decision he and the principal had agreed to: Aiden was welcome back as soon as one of his parents could bring him to school and attend a meeting. "I want to visit with you and Aiden before he comes back to class," Mr. Harrison said. "He doesn't have to stay out of school any time at all if you can meet with me at seven-thirty tomorrow morning," he added. "And I

LOVE AND LOGIC EXPERIMENT:
Delaying the Consequence

TEACHER: "Will you talk quietly as we walk in the hall? Will you do that just for me? Thanks."

STUDENT (with a very snotty tone): "Thanks is something you say after somebody does what you ask. I just laugh at people who say that first. You can't tell me how to talk."

TEACHER (as calmly as possibly under the circumstances): "Oh... no problem... I'm going to have to do something about this. We'll talk later."

STUDENT (defiantly): "So."

TEACHER (walks away reminding himself): This is not the time to deal with this. It's okay if she thinks she's gotten away with this in the short term.

don't want to make this a bigger problem for you than it already is. We're hoping we can simply handle this with Aiden at school."

What will establish the greatest ongoing level of respect between Aiden and Mr. Harrison? Will it be to expect his mother to solve this problem? Or will it involve Mr. Harrison showing that he is willing and able to work this out directly with Aiden? We see a theme here:

Healthy Human Dynamics 101:
When Person A has a problem with Person B,
they must work it out directly with Person B.

Person C can provide ideas and mediation,
but they must remain out of the middle.

Mom and Aiden were there promptly at 7:30 a.m. Obviously, Mom was upset. "I suppose he'll have in-school suspension now. That's what all of his other teachers do! Last year he was there almost every day."

After a great deal of listening and showing that he cared, Mr. Harrison asked, "Would you like to hear how I handle things a bit differently in my classroom?"

Mom nodded, "Okay. How are you different?"

Mr. Harrison described his approach: "I try to treat each student as a unique person, and each situation as a unique situation. I encourage each individual student to solve their problems in ways that don't create problems for anyone else. Maybe you'd like to look at my rules and my guarantee to the kids. I told them that I treat each situation on a case-by-case basis. I also took time to teach them how to have an informal due process meeting. In other words, they get to share their side of the story. Right here is my written guarantee. If they present a good case I may be willing to change what I do."

"So why did you make him leave school yesterday?" Mom asked.

"Is that what he told you?" Mr. Harrison asked with surprise.

Mom nodded, "Yeah, he said he got kicked out of school because Gabriel was talking trash."

"Aiden?" Mr. Harrison grinned, turning to the teen. "This is confusing. Why do you think, even though I've given you a written guarantee to listen to your side of a story, you still chose to leave school?"

Aiden slid a bit farther into his chair. "I don't know… 'cuz teachers never listen."

Continuing to smile, Mr. Harrison replied, "Well, I'm just a different kind of teacher. I'm willing to listen as long as I see that you are working hard to solve this problem in a way that doesn't make a problem for anyone else."

"How am I supposed to do that?" Aiden asked.

"I'm not sure," Mr. Harrison admitted, "but I think we ought to help you stay out of hassles with 'G' by having you spend the day in the office. That will give you some time to think about how to solve the problem."

"Is that in-school suspension?" Aiden's mother asked.

Mr. Harrison answered, "No. It's just a quiet place for Aiden to make a plan for staying out of hassles with Gabriel. My goal is always to help students stay out of trouble... rather than punishing them."

Aiden's mother paused. Then she turned to her son. "Well, he's had problems with that kid before, but I don't know if he wants to talk about it or not... But, I know one thing for sure... Aiden... you look at me when I'm talking to you! I think you need to start listening to this man!" With that, she grabbed her purse and headed for the door.

Traditional Systems Appear to Work... for the Students Who Don't Need Them

During the first few years of his teaching career, Mr. Harrison and his colleagues relied on the traditional approach to classroom and school discipline. This involved lots of meetings with other staff members where they diligently worked toward some key goals:

- Identify a list of typical misbehaviors performed by students (a.k.a. "infractions").
- Make clear rules against doing such things.
- Craft consequences for each and every infraction.
- Develop successively more severe consequences for students who break the same rule more than once.
- Write all of this down and put it in a handbook.
- Laminate copies of the rules and consequences, and then post them for the world to see.

Mr. Harrison and the other teachers at his school believed that this approach would ensure consistency. Each staff member would handle all of the rules and all of the consequences according to the book... in exactly the same way. Defending their actions to parents would be easier. Students would be aware of the danger of violating rules, know what to expect if they did, and therefore, be much better behaved.

It was a wonderful dream… while it lasted.

Their system was working really well. That is with compliant students who didn't need a behavior management system.

The problem was that the more challenging kids were not playing along. They were breaking rules anyway and even doing so incorrectly. That's right! They seemed to delight in breaking the rules just off center… in new and creative ways… so the prescribed consequences no longer seemed to fit. Then they'd act like lawyers, arguing, "Well, I didn't do *that*."

Even more shocking was that many brought their parents along as co-council! Mr. Harrison and his peers were also hearing from them: "Well… he/she didn't do *that!*" Their new and wonderful discipline system seemed to awaken a once silent battalion of hostile helicopter parents.

Bad ideas die hard. Just because these systems have been proven ineffective with difficult students… time and time again… it doesn't mean we abandon them. It simply means we have more staff meetings designed to rectify the "slight flaws" in our system.

Mr. Harrison and the team identified more rules and more severe consequences. They added these to the list, printed a new workbook, and laminated some new posters. All of this was based on two faulty assumptions:

1. If students know exactly what kind of consequences they will face when rules are broken, they won't break the rules.

2. If students continue to act out, it's due to one or more of the following:

   a. We don't have enough rules.

   b. Our consequences aren't severe enough.

   c. Administrators or other teachers aren't enforcing the consequences consistently.

d. Administrators are letting parents rescue their kids from the consequences.

The Truth: More Rules Will Never Solve the Problem

There's a classic example in one of our books about Brad, a creative student who brought a dead fish to school and rubbed it in a girl's hair. When told that it was against the rules, he argued, "My dad and I read all the rules in the discipline policy and not one of them says anything about a dead fish."

Believe it or not, the school made a new rule to cover that eventuality. It had to do with fish, but before long he did it again, this time with a dead salamander. I'm sure you know what his argument was this time: "A salamander is not a fish, and the rule says fish."

Had this school adopted the Love and Logic approach, the rules would have been limited, but inclusive:

Feel free to do whatever you would like as long as it doesn't cause a problem.

Obviously Brad's action created a problem for the girl. In a Love and Logic school, Brad would have heard, "Around here, people who create problems are expected to solve those problems without making a problem for anyone else, including their own parents. How do you plan on doing that? I have a nice quiet place for you to work on a solution, and as soon as you have an acceptable one, I will consider letting you return to your classwork."

There would be no need for another staff meeting spent attempting to develop new and better rules. The adults in the school would be doing very little thinking about the problem. Brad would be doing a lot.

If the principal felt a bit devilish, he might even say something akin to: "Now, Brad, there's no need to hurry. We offer your grade every year at this school, so it's not like you'll miss out on anything."

Why Traditional Systems Fail:
How Our Most Challenging Students Think

Mr. Harrison and his more astute colleagues gradually began to grieve the loss of their beloved golden calf. This came as their eyes opened to the massive mismatch between their traditional system and the psychological and social realities of the challenging students it was intended to help. Clearer and clearer became the tragic ineffectiveness of trying to manage these students in traditional ways.

Win-Lose Orientation

Effective educators, and other helping professionals, tend to view the world as a win-win place. As such, they do not view their list of consequences as threats. They view it as a nice way of helping students stay out of trouble.

Our most challenging students see it quite differently. Why? Some were born that way. Because of normal genetic variation, they left the womb smoking cigars and wearing little red boxing gloves. Their basic orientation has been to question authority and to fight anything that might leave them feeling a lesser sense of control. When they sense threat, they react with, "You want a piece of me? Let's see if you can really make that happen!"

Negative Interpretive Bias and
High Baseline Levels of Arousal

Others act this way because they've learned that the only way to survive is to fight tooth and nail for what they want. Many have survived emotionally… and often physically… by seeing everything as threatening and by reacting quickly. Because of this, their brains are constantly flooded with adrenaline and cortisol. This neurochemical soup makes it even more likely that our efforts to help by listing consequences, will result in battles rather than the calm classrooms we desire.

Consequences as a Badge of Honor

If these students know exactly what consequence will happen when they break specific rules, they often do an informal, subconscious cost-benefit analysis. They compare the potential discomfort associated with the consequence with the badge of honor they will receive from failing to be intimidated by threats provided by adults. Unfortunately, they often conclude that testing the threat and experiencing the consequence is worth it.

Similarly, many schools place these students in a bind by implementing rigid reward systems where the goal is to catch students being good so that praise and rewards can be provided. While these systems look great at first glance, there are some similar side effects when it comes to troubled students. Public rewards and praise often leave these students no choice: Once they receive them, they are forced to act out in order to prove they are not the "teachers' pets."

For decades, educators have confirmed these concerns by providing example after example of tough students self-destructing after being praised or receiving a reward. A far more powerful strategy involves building sincere relationships with these students, where we carefully avoid embarrassing them while noticing what is unique and positive about them apart from the school behavior or academic performance. (See the one-sentence intervention in chapter 3)

Entitlement Mentality

"You owe me!"

Entitlement is a strange beast, largely because it's born from two possible origins. The first source is the one most of us typically imagine when we consider the term "entitled child." We imagine a student who suffers from "under-expectation and over-indulgence syndrome." The child runs the home, is rescued from each poor decision, and is given all the perks of success without having to exert a single drop of perspiration. There are plenty of these students... from all socioeconomic and ethnic backgrounds.

The second source looks completely different. Here we have a student who's experienced chronic mistreatment in the form of neglect, abuse, or both. Because of the great hurt they've experienced, they believe that it is now their turn: "The world owes me because of all that I've been through." For different reasons, some of these students also exhibit the key hallmarks of entitlement. The most relevant to our current discussion include:

- Unwilling to take responsibility for their actions.
- Constantly manipulates by lying, deceiving, or pushing buttons.
- Pits others against each other to gain control of the environment.

There are few things that give entitled students more unhealthy power over adults than lists of consequences. They break the rules in unexpected and creative ways, they relentlessly manipulate to evade consequences, and they watch with great satisfaction as parents blame teachers, teachers blame parents, and educators blame each other. Divide and conquer is their modus operandi.

Much of the ineffectiveness of traditional disciplinary systems can be understood according to the "Threat Cycle," originally discussed by Dr. Raymond Wlodkowski in his book, *Teaching and Motivation*. This cycle is a powerful way of predicting the behavior of many people when they sense a threat.

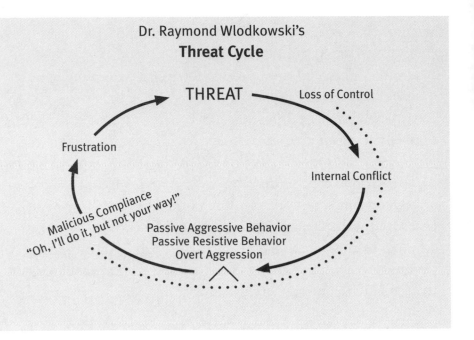

As they develop a sense of potential loss of control they face internal conflicts, often leading to passive-aggressive, passive-resistive, or overtly aggressive behavior.

In the event that they see themselves possibly facing total loss of control, they regain it through malicious compliance: "Okay, I'll do it, but not your way." For example, a student is ordered to the office, and she walks so slowly that you have to compare her to stationary objects to know she is actually moving.

The Silent Tragedy of Traditional Systems: How Compliant Students Feel

It should also be remembered that threats seem to work well with the population of kids we don't need to scare… that is, the well-behaved students. In reality, they tend to backfire by increasing the anxiety levels of these well-behaved students. Since we know that excess anxiety impairs learning and performance, is this really the way we want these kids to experience life at school?

No Two Educators Are Alike

Traditional systems were largely developed to create consistency among staff. The logic goes as follows: "If every rule and consequence is set in stone, teachers will treat every student and every situation in the same way."

Is this reality… or is perception reality?

Mr. Jackson sees Festus running down the hall and thinks, *I wish I could still run like that.* He's happy for Festus and doesn't perceive a rule infraction.

Mrs. Henson witnesses the same thing and thinks, *That's a criminal offense and I'd better put a stop to it.* She comes down hard on the offender.

Mr. Jackson watches Mrs. Henson's actions and thinks, *The trouble with this school is those uptight people like Mrs. Henson. She needs to loosen up a little. The kid wasn't running that fast in the first place.*

Mrs. Henson sees Mr. Jackson's lack of action and thinks, *No wonder we have discipline problems around this school. Nobody enforces the rules.*

It wasn't long before there was a morale problem. And you guessed it: a faculty meeting held to discuss consistency. How can we get everybody to enforce the rules the same way?

Some common mantras were voiced: "If the other teachers would just enforce the rules the way they should, I wouldn't be having discipline problems." Another frequent theme was: "If the other teachers would just loosen up and stay off of these kids' backs there wouldn't be so many problems around here."

Isn't it interesting that we tend to blame each other for the failure of the system rather than considering that the system may have some fatal flaws?

Traditional systems backfire because:

1. challenging students view these as threats.
2. it gives them time to brace themselves for the prescribed consequences.
3. many are compelled to test the resolve of the adult.
4. they have time to think of ways to violate the rule in a slightly different way so they can argue about fairness, etc.
5. they often orchestrate arguments between the parents and the teacher in attempts to defend their positions.
6. staff blame each other for the failure of the system.
7. students often view consequences as a badge of honor.
8. such threats often create perceptions of control loss.
9. loss of control often stimulates manipulative and/or resistive behaviors.

The Solution: Guiding Principles... Not a Step-by-Step System

Is it possible to have the best of both worlds where we achieve consistency in the way we handle management and discipline challenges and avoid the problems associated with traditional classroom and school discipline plans?

Yes! It all comes down to combining a core set of principles with some practical and powerful Love and Logic techniques. Like a compass, the principles give us the direction in which we yearn to go with all students. Like our car, the practical techniques provide the specific tools for getting there.

The Core Principles of the Love and Logic Approach

Love and Logic is based on five nonnegotiable principles. These serve to keep our attention and actions consistent with the mission... while providing enough freedom to meet the unique needs of individual students and situations. As we consider how we manage our classrooms and provide student discipline, our question is not, How can I follow "the system." Rather, it's whether the actions I'm about to take are consistent with the foundational values of Love and Logic.

PRINCIPLE ONE: MUTUAL DIGNITY AND RESPECT

Am I prepared to provide this management or disciplinary intervention in a way that demonstrates respect toward my students and maintains their dignity?

How will I take good care of myself so that I don't allow my students to treat me like a doormat?

PRINCIPLE TWO: SINCERE EMPATHY

How will I communicate a strong dose of genuine understanding and compassion prior to expecting students to solve the problems they create? Will I be capable of providing consequences preceded by sincere empathy rather than providing them with anger, lectures, threats, or sarcasm?

PRINCIPLE THREE: SHARED THINKING

Will I be doing most of the thinking? Or will my student(s) have to? Am I primarily focused on thinking about consequences for my students, or am I leaning mostly toward guiding them to own and solve the problems they create?

PRINCIPLE FOUR: SHARED CONTROL WITHIN LIMITS

Am I making all of the decisions for my students, or am I allowing them to decide the smaller things that don't affect the welfare of others? Am I remembering that we all have strong needs for control?

PRINCIPLE FIVE: IT ALL POINTS TO HEALTHY RELATIONSHIPS

Am I establishing myself as a caring authority figure? Will this intervention build or maintain a relationship with the student(s)

Thinking Words versus Fighting Words

In many classrooms, setting limits means issuing commands. Love and Logic teachers ask questions and offer choices instead, which places the responsibility for decision making on the students.

Fighting Words: "If you don't stop teasing those kids during recess, you're getting recess detention."
Thinking Words: "I allow students to enjoy the playground when I don't have to worry about how they treat others while using it."

****

Fighting Words: "Keep your hands to yourself. That's disruptive."
Thinking Words: "Feel free to sit next to each other as long doing so doesn't cause any problems."

****

Fighting Words: "You need to get to work."
Thinking Words: "I like students the same regardless of how high or low their grade ends up being. Please let me know how I can help."

where I am viewed as powerful and compassionate at the very same time? Am I remembering that challenging students need strong teachers who are friendly… not friendly teachers who are pushovers?

Love and Logic: A Menu of Practical Techniques

The core principles give us the direction. The practical tools give us strategies for getting there. As you continue through the pages of this book, you'll discover a variety of specific techniques guaranteed to change your life… not just with your students but other people in your life. This guarantee is real. If this book doesn't change your life, we'll gladly buy it back.

In chapter one, Lynne discovered that the one-sentence intervention and short-term recovery breathed life into her teaching career. She also discovered the tremendous power of whispering. In this chapter you saw how Mr. Harrison used *How I Run my Love and Logic Classroom* to turn a potentially disastrous situation into an opportunity to build a relationship with a tough student and a challenging parent. In your classroom, we believe you'll see the power of these positive and life-changing skills. Enjoy!

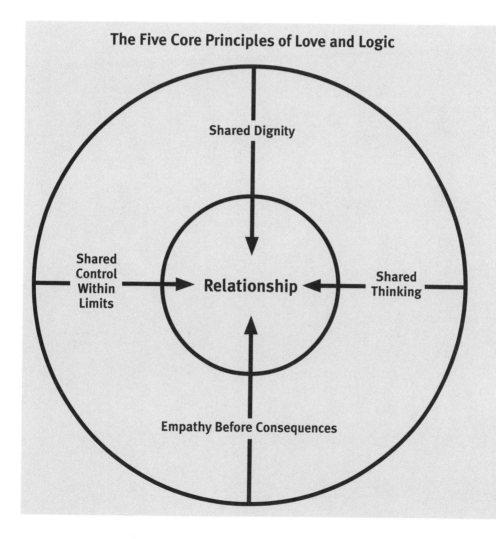

The Five Core Principles of Love and Logic

Shared Dignity

Shared Control Within Limits → Relationship ← Shared Thinking

Empathy Before Consequences

Gaining Their Admiration and Respect

I (Jim) was hoodwinked. Yes, I was tricked by my very own mother. She tricked me into believing she could make me do everything that she told me to do.

Mom was a small woman, so before long my brothers and I were all bigger and stronger than she was. But still, we believed she could make us do anything she told us to do. How could this be? Many of my teenage friends didn't have that same feeling. They knew that nobody could make them do something they didn't want to do, and they acted accordingly, acting defiantly and arguing with their parents over everything they didn't want to do.

What's the first step toward gaining our students' admiration and respect? How do we lovingly leave them believing that we are one of the most powerful people on the planet? Is it by trying to be their friend? No. Is it by barking orders and issuing threats with more gusto than the teacher next-door? Nope. It's by doing what my mother did on a consistent basis: She proved that her "yes" always meant "yes" and her "no" always meant "no."

Her "yes" was always "yes" and her "no" was always "no."

My mother was a master at setting limits for my brothers and me. As such, we never doubted her word. You could take everything she said to the bank and cash it in for pure gold. That meant she never weakened her credibility by telling us to do something she couldn't make happen two hundred percent of the time. As a result, Mom was the undisputed... and dearly loved, authority figure in our home.

She maintained her credibility by never... ever... setting a limit she couldn't enforce.

How to Start a Fight You'll Never Win: Use "Fighting Words"

Somehow our mother had developed some major wisdom. While lacking much of a formal education, she knew what a lot of people without graduate degrees don't understand: When you tell a stubborn person what they should or should not do, it almost always starts an unwinnable fight.

Many educators and parents find themselves embroiled in constant power struggles because they've fallen into the habit of telling kids what to do. While they believe they're setting limits, they're really not. Let's consider what happens... psychologically... when you tell a stubborn person what to do or not do:

Step One: A warning sounds in their subconscious mind: "Control loss! You're losing control! You can't let that happen."

Step Two: They consider some options for regaining control:
- Hearing loss.
- Memory impairment.
- Passive resistance or aggression. (Do what you're told... but do it sloppily, or in way that creates a bigger problem for the person who's trying to boss you around.)
- Do exactly the opposite of what you've been told.

Step Three: Enjoy the feelings of great power as you watch the veins on the other person's forehead bulge.

When this happens to a well-meaning teacher who simply wants her students to keep their hands to themselves and stop being disruptive, any of the above "options for regaining control" create a major inconvenience. Unfortunately, that's not the worst part. The most destructive aspect of this scenario has to do with what happens to this teacher's credibility, or authority in their students' eyes.

When we tell a stubborn student what to do, how long does it take them to prove that we are completely powerless? How long does it take after we tell a stubborn kid what to do for them to prove to themselves and anyone witnessing, that we have absolutely no strength or authority?

I (Charles) had an experience that drove this point home. There I was, driving in the car with my son. He was seventeen at the time and was experiencing a season of snits. For some reason, he was constantly bent out of shape about one thing or the other. About 3.5 minutes into the drive, he's making nasty comments about other drivers, the weather, and the general order of the universe.

Have you ever experienced skill slippage?

Irritated and somehow ready to fight a battle I could never win, I turned to him and lectured, "Watch your mouth!"

At the precise second it came out of my mouth, I knew it wasn't the most loving and logical way to handle the problem. This was confirmed when he defiantly flipped down the sun visor and looked dramatically into the vanity mirror… "I'm watching my mouth," he proclaimed with great sarcasm.

How long did it take for him to prove himself and to me that I lacked the power to directly control what came out of his mouth? If this sort of thing were to happen on a rather consistent basis, how long would it take before he learned to ignore just about everything that came out of my mouth? It might have been far more effective for me to say something like, "Oh, son, I'm always happy to drive you the places you want to go when I don't have to worry about hearing negative comments. And… by the way… I'm always happy to allow kids to use the family car when I'm feeling respected."

The more we try to make someone change,
the more likely we are to lock him or her
into the offending behavior.

Let's consider a classroom example, where the well-meaning teacher mentioned above says to a couple of strong-willed eighth graders: "Keep your hands to yourself." What are the odds that this teacher will soon be seen as completely powerless by these two students and the entire class? After the fighting words, "Keep your hands to yourself" enter her students' ear canals, how many milliseconds will it take for them to begin touching each other more intensely? That's how long it takes for us to lose our power when we tell stubborn kids (and even adults) what to do.

Would this teacher enjoy a more positive result if he or she wandered over to these students and said something like, "I allow students to sit where they like as long as it doesn't cause a problem." Even if the kids don't immediately comply, she doesn't look powerless. In fact, she might allow them to think they've gotten away with being noncompliant. That is, until the next time class meets when these students discover they now have seats on opposite sides of the room.

Mom Used Thinking Words, Instead

My (Jim's) mom rarely told us what to do. Instead, she told us what she was going to do. As a result, we found ourselves having to think hard about how we were going to successfully fit into the way she ran her own life. We were constantly forced to consider our own behavior as she described hers: "I listen when kids are talking respectfully. I wash clothes that are placed in the hamper. I take kids places when they are finished with their chores. I offer dinner until seven p.m."

> **LOVE AND LOGIC EXPERIMENT:**
> ## Bothering Others
>
> STUDENT: (Student is visiting or bothering others when she should be working.)
>
> TEACHER (whispering with a grin): "Could you save that for Mr. Thompson's class? He really likes that stuff. Thanks." (Turn your back and walk away without waiting for an answer.)

My brothers and I share an early memory of Mother Marie sweetly informing us that she'd be serving dinner in twenty minutes... and that she'd provide a place setting for those with clean hands. Just about that time we were distracted by the sound of a fire truck roaring down the street. Bursting out of the front door, the three of us raced down the block to see what was going on. We forgot about dinner. Returning an hour later, we found the food in the refrigerator. It was cold. As you can imagine, the cold mashed potatoes and gravy caused us to think deeply.

It was at that time we all decided that listening to Mom was a wise thing to do. We were starting to realize that ignoring her always resulted in a problem for us, not for her. Since she never told us in advance what the problem was going to be, we couldn't conduct a cost/benefit analysis and were forced to do some major thinking.

At some point in her young life, our mother must have discovered that the only person she could control was herself. As such, she spent little or no time trying to control us. Ironically, this forced us to work hard on controlling ourselves.

When we spend less time trying to control others, we have more time and energy to provide great role modeling.

Thinking Words Create "Enforceable Statements"

Mom could enforce her limits because she only told us what she was going to do. Her enforceable statements established limits and boundaries for her kids.

Instead of saying, "Don't talk to me in that tone of voice," she'd say, "I'll listen when your voice sounds calm like mine."

Instead of saying, "I'm not doing this homework for you," she'd say, "I'll help with your homework when I see that you are doing more work than I am."

She didn't order, "Hurry up!" but calmly let us know, "My car is leaving in thirty minutes."

She didn't say, "I'm not buying you that. Put it back on the shelf," but instead she said, "Feel free to have that when you can afford it."

She didn't say, "Show a little respect," but rather, "I'm happy to do the things you want when I feel respected and your chores are done."

She didn't demand, "Get your chores done," but simply said, "I'll drive you to baseball practice as soon as your chores are done."

She didn't nag, "Come on. Get up. Get out of bed. For crying out loud," but rather informed us, "Here is your one and only wake-up call."

"Thinking Words" in the Classroom

Practically all teachers begin their careers knowing their ability to set and enforce limits is important. Many of us, however, encounter students who give us an inaccurate perspective as how to actually make it happen. Too frequently, we meet just enough compliant students to convince us that telling kids what to do is effective. To these docile students, we say, "Pay attention," and they pay attention. We say, "Settle down," and they settle down. We say, "Keep your hands to yourself," and... you guessed it... they actually comply. These sweet students, with all of their compliant behavior, do us a great disservice by deluding us into thinking we can actually control the behavior of others.

When we believe that old techniques would work if students would just behave, we have a discipline problem that's too difficult to solve.

Fortunately, we all eventually meet students who are willing to give us a more accurate perspective as to how much power we really have over others. These wonderful, obstinate, strong-willed young people provide salient learning opportunities that motivate us to find more effective techniques. Let's imagine a student who came out of the womb smoking a cigar, wearing little red boxing gloves, and talking like James Cagney in those old gangster movies: "Hey, Doc. Before ya cut dat cord, let's get straight with who's da boss here …ay!"

Which of the following will get us the most favorable result?

UNENFORCEABLE STATEMENT "Fighting Words"	ENFORCEABLE STATEMENT "Thinking Words"
Hand your papers in on time.	I assign full credit to papers handed in on time.
Quit texting. Give me your cell phone.	Cell phones are great. I allow them to remain in the room as long as they aren't causing a problem.
Stop visiting with each other.	Feel free to visit as long as it's done quietly.
Get to work.	I'm always willing to help. Please let me know if you are interested.
You need to get a better attitude.	I'll listen when your voice is calm like mine.
You are not joining us for the activity until you have that cleaned up.	Feel free to join us as soon as that's all put away.
Turn to page six.	I'm currently on page six.

Walk! Stop running in the hall.	I'm concerned about you. I allow students to continue when I see that they can walk.
You keep causing disruptions. You need to get yourself together.	I allow students to remain with the group as long as they aren't causing a problem.
You need to behave in the cafeteria.	We allow students to use the cafeteria when they can do so without causing a problem. Ms. Jones has a nice quiet place for you to eat lunch until you've come up with a plan.
Take that hat off. That's not dress code.	It's great to see you. I allow students to join us when I see they have their hats off.

The enforceable statements provided above are simply examples. Wise educators never leap blindly into anything until they've considered how well it fits their unique students and their unique personalities. The key point is not that you use exactly what's written in the pages of this book. No. Far more important is that you develop a rather small number of limits that you know... beyond a shadow of a doubt... you can enforce without breaking a sweat.

To create their own enforceable statements, many educators find it helpful to use the following generic format:

"I allow_____, as long as it doesn't cause a problem."

For example, "I allow *students to work in groups on this task* as long as it doesn't cause a problem." Or, "I allow *students to use the internet to research this* as long as it doesn't cause a problem." Or perhaps, "I allow *students to do their work standing, sitting, kneeling, or in any other physical position* as long as it doesn't cause a problem."

Successful Educators Set Relatively Few Limits

We are huge advocates of setting limits with kids. In fact, we're huge advocates of setting limits and boundaries with all people, regardless of age. With this said, please don't fall into the trap of thinking you need a mile-long list. The most successful educators intensify their focus on a relatively small number of limits. Then they prove to their students that they can enforce them without shedding a single drop of perspiration. Less successful people, in contrast, attempt to set and enforce too many. Spread too thin and seeming incredibly uptight, they quickly lose their authority and their students' respect.

> **LOVE AND LOGIC EXPERIMENT:**
> ### Not Following Rules
>
> STUDENT: (Not following the rules during a game.)
>
> TEACHER: "There are two ways to enjoy the game. One, is by playing it, and the other one, is by watching it. Which would you rather do?"
>
> STUDENT: "Well, I'm not the only one..."
>
> TEACHER (with empathy): "Oh, man. It looks like you'll be watching."
>
> STUDENT: "Not fair!"
>
> TEACHER: "I bet it looks that way, and you may return to the game when I don't have to worry about cheating and arguing."

Do Our Students Thank Us for the Limits We Set?

I (Charles) watched a teacher use a powerful enforceable statement with one of the most difficult students in her school. Leaning into his ear, she whispered, "I allow students to remain with the group when they aren't making calls on their cell phone."

This amazingly tough kid gazed her way and replied, "This is... amazing! I feel so much better now that I know that you care enough to set limits. Will you please take my phone so I'm not tempted to use it during class? And, teacher... would it be okay if I gave you a hug?"

The student handed her the phone and hugged her. Tears of joy streamed down his cheeks.

Then I woke up. It was a pleasant dream while it lasted.

What's the eyes open and wide-awake reality of setting effective limits with tough students? They'll almost always test to see if our limits are real… and if we care enough and are strong enough to enforce them.

> *Kids yearn for the very same limits*
> *they argue with us about the most.*

> *It's our job to set limits.*

> *It's a kid's job to test these limits.*

If we love our students enough to set limits, we'd better expect them to test us by arguing, whining, and trying to manipulate their way around these limits. This doesn't mean they are bad kids, it simply means they need to see if we are strong and caring enough to hold our ground.

QUESTION: If students are able to wear us down by arguing over the limits we set, do we really have effective limits?

QUESTION: Who's really in control when a student successfully pulls us into a debate over a limit we have set?

QUESTION: Do we remain a loving authority figure under such circumstances, or are we seen by students as weak and unable to lead?

Visiting with her friends in the workroom at West Mountain Middle School, Sandy complained, "I don't know what's wrong with kids today. Even the smallest request or limit ends up getting me a load of back talk. I tell them not to talk to me that way, but it just seems to make things worse."

This stimulated a rather lively discussion.

Vickie replied, "Oh, I had the same problem at home with my teenager, Paul. He argues with everything I say."

Bree agreed: "Just today I had a student tell me that I couldn't make her do an assignment because it wasn't in her IEP. I couldn't believe it. I tried to explain to her that it was something she needed in order to understand the next part of the subject, but she just kept arguing."

"Yeah, I get that kind of back talk, too," responded Veronica. "A boy in one of my classes told me that because he forgot to take his medication it wasn't his fault he hit a kid. When I got home that very same day, my son told me that he wasn't going to take out the trash."

When a Child Starts to Argue, go "Brain Dead"

Too frequently we try to match wits with arguing kids. We attempt to do so by using our superior wisdom and logic to change their minds. Have you ever seen this work? Have you ever seen a stubborn student, after being lectured about the importance of completing his work, turn to the teacher and say, "I totally disagreed with what you said until you mentioned the part about me having a really hard life if I don't get an education. That makes so much sense. Thanks for sharing your wisdom. I better get to work."

When kids argue with adults, they couldn't care less about wisdom and logic. Their goal is to simply get their way… or to at least see the color of the adult's face turn an exciting hue of red.

For this reason, wise teachers remember to go "brain dead" as soon as they sense an argument coming their way. They remind themselves, "Don't think too hard about what this kid is saying or doing. If I do I'll be tempted to either reason or make a threat I can't back up." These highly skilled people understand that reasoning with an angry, arguing child is like fighting a fire with gasoline. Every word used simply heaps more fuel on the inferno.

Every effort made to correct the student erodes their view of us as a strong and caring leader.

***Teachers who get pulled into reasoning with
arguing students commit leadership suicide.***

It's important for all of us to remember that many children have been practicing their manipulation skills for years before they enter our classrooms. Many have already mastered the art of getting what they want by hooking their parents into unwinnable arguments. Their parents have fallen into the trap of trying to reason with them, only finding that every attempt to do so only stimulates more arguing.

These children are adept at twisting their parents' words into "bird walk" after "bird walk" until the frustrated parent eventually gives in. It is not long before these children believe that getting one's way is simply a matter of wearing down adults.

There are few things more damaging than allowing kids to believe they can use arguing or manipulation to get their way, to push others' buttons, or to deflect responsibility for their poor decisions.

When this happens it has a powerfully negative impact on the adult's ability to remain a healthy authority figure. The adult…

- is no longer seen by the child as a compelling role model.
- becomes unable to establish limits, boundaries, or any other type of positive discipline. (Every attempt they make to use a new skill is met with massive back talk.)
- begins to set fewer necessary limits in a subconscious attempt to avoid hassles from the kids. (i.e.: The kids train the adults to stay out of their way.)
- starts to dislike the child and begins to come across as bitter or resentful.
- often experiences serious burn-out and depression.

Obviously this also has a massively negative effect on the child. They…

- begin to act out even more in a subconscious attempt to find the security found in limits.
- lose opportunities to learn from their poor decisions.
- become susceptible to beliefs of entitlement.
- rarely learn delayed gratification or other forms of self-control.
- fail to develop a healthy view of authority figures.
- become addicted to the drama of arguing and manipulation.
- often suffer from chronic feelings of hostility toward adults and themselves.

LOVE AND LOGIC EXPERIMENT:

When Do I Argue?

STUDENT: (Student is trying to argue.)

TEACHER (smiles): "When do I argue?"

STUDENT: "Yeah, but it's not fair."

TEACHER (pointing at a sign on the wall): "I argue at 12:15 and 3:15 daily. What's best for you?"

STUDENT: "Yeah, but that's at lunch and after school."

TEACHER (still smiling): "I know."

Based on the above, we shouldn't be surprised that so many students enter our classrooms primed to challenge our necessary position as a caring authority figure. Fortunately, we can turn this situation around… at least in our classroom… when we remember two things:

Number One: When a student starts to argue, go "brain dead."
Number Two: Calmly repeat your Love and Logic "one-liner." And begin to move away from the student.

Love and Logic "One-Liners"

We've established the importance of going "brain dead" so we can remain calmer and resist the urge to reason with the arguing student. What comes next? Listed below are just a few favorite Love and Logic "one-liners" used by teachers all over the world. The key to success is not using all of them. It's selecting one, or creating one of your own, and using the same one over and over again, regardless of what the student says.

- I know.
- I care about you (or respect you) too much to argue.
- Thanks for sharing... and what did I say?
- Could be... and what did I say?
- When do I argue? (during lunch and after school)
- Ohhhh...

LET'S CONSIDER A QUICK EXAMPLE:

TEACHER (with sincere empathy): "This is such a bummer. I see that you were using your tablet to watch videos instead of doing your work. When do I allow students to use the web for research?"

STUDENT: "I got on that website on accident. It wasn't my fault! Not fair."

TEACHER (with a sincere, compassionate smile and remembering to go "brain dead"): "What did I say?"

STUDENT: "I'm telling my dad. He's a lawyer! It's your fault if I fail this project!"

TEACHER (still calm and empathetic): "And what did I say?"

STUDENT: "You're not even listening to me! You don't care."

TEACHER (resisting the urge to lecture or get emotional): "And what did I say?"

STUDENT: "I won't do it again... I promise... Give me another chance..."

TEACHER (moving away from the student): "And what did I say?"

When Kids Try to Argue

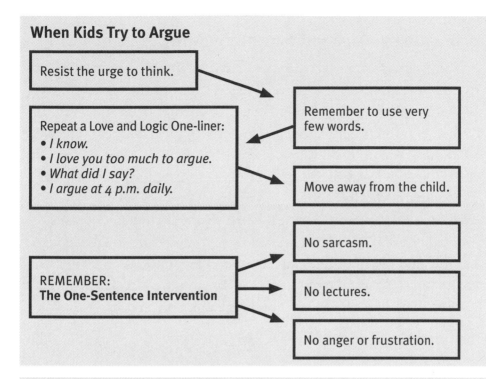

Resist the urge to think.

Repeat a Love and Logic One-liner:
- *I know.*
- *I love you too much to argue.*
- *What did I say?*
- *I argue at 4 p.m. daily.*

Remember to use very few words.

Move away from the child.

REMEMBER:
The One-Sentence Intervention

No sarcasm.

No lectures.

No anger or frustration.

The One-Sentence Intervention

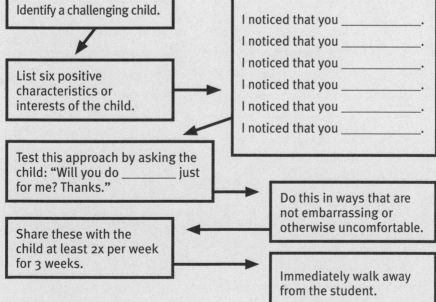

Identify a challenging child.

List six positive characteristics or interests of the child.

Test this approach by asking the child: "Will you do _____ just for me? Thanks."

Share these with the child at least 2x per week for 3 weeks.

I noticed that you _____.
I noticed that you _____.
I noticed that you _____.
I noticed that you _____.
I noticed that you _____.
I noticed that you _____.

Do this in ways that are not embarrassing or otherwise uncomfortable.

Immediately walk away from the student.

One-Liners: Done with Empathy or with Sarcasm?

Some educators make the grave error of thinking that using one-liners is a way to get even with students or to somehow put them in their place. Nothing could be further from the truth. In fact, one-liners delivered with sarcasm or anger are guaranteed to make the problem worse.

The kids loved Mr. Elias... one of the toughest teachers at West Mountain Middle School. He was tough because his limits were firm and he always expected the best from his students. He was loved by them, because he knew how to combine this toughness with great amounts of sincere empathy and kind humor. Overhearing his colleagues discuss their woes with argumentative kids, he described something he'd learned at a Love and Logic conference:

> *"As a young teacher, I used to have a lot of trouble with students talking back and arguing. Then I had an opportunity to hear Jim Fay speak. He taught mostly with stories, and the one that made me think was about a teacher who made a sign for her classroom. Anytime a student would argue, she'd smile in a friendly way, point to the sign, and ask, 'When do I argue?' The sign read, 'I argue with students at 11:15 a.m. and 3:15 p.m. daily.' At her school, this was during student lunch and after school. Any time they brought this fact to her attention, she'd empathize, 'I know, and when do I argue?'"*

Mr. Elias continued by describing how he modified it for his classroom:

> *"When my students try to argue, I just smile and ask them to make an appointment. I've also let them know that if they present a respectful disagreement and a good case, I might make some changes. They rarely take advantage of*

this opportunity, but when they do, I always find it improves our relationship."

When it comes to neutralizing student arguing, every effective teacher has a slightly different approach. What we say in response to arguments is not nearly as important as establishing the fact that every time it happens, we respond in a predictably firm, yet empathetic way. One teacher commented:

"I began to realize that if I used any words... any words at all... my students would throw them back at me. Then I'd find myself getting frustrated. One day, when I was at a complete loss for how to respond, I accidentally replied with 'Ohh.' Actually it was an empathetic, drawn-out 'Ohhhhhhh' where I simply let all of the air out of my lungs. I couldn't believe it. The kid actually paused. I think he was confused. Then I kept repeating, 'Ohhhhhh.' He quickly gave up, walked back to his desk, and plunked himself into his chair. Now 'Ohhhhhh' is my go-to response when they begin to argue. I've made it so predictable that now they beat me to it, and often say, 'Oh... I know... ohhhhh,' and walk away. What I love about this one-liner is that it fits anything a kid might say, it helps me stay calm, and I can't produce words when there is no air in my lungs."

Mutual Dignity

Perhaps we should examine how all of this fits with the Five Principles of Love and Logic, the first being mutual dignity. How would you like to be spoken to? Are we maintaining a student's dignity when we bark orders, always telling them what they should do or not do? Do we show great respect when we try to match wits with students by trying to argue our point?

Does any of this bring the best out of anyone? In contrast, do we use the language of dignity and respect when we assertively describe what we are going to do or allow… and calmly demonstrate that we care about them too much to argue?

During a presentation by our good friend and colleague, Dave Funk, one rather confrontational participant shouted, "Well, Mr. Funk, you keep talking about words of respect. How are we supposed to know what these words are?"

"Oh," he answered, "I bet you already know the words of respect. They are the ones you use with your class while your principal and school superintendent are sitting in the back of the room."

Love and Logic emphasizes dignity provided to students, but it also places a heavy emphasis on teachers maintaining their own dignity. When we are able to set and enforce limits without threats, lectures, or arguments, do we maintain our own dignity and self-respect?

Shared Thinking and Shared Control Within Limits

Two additional and closely related Love and Logic principles are shared thinking and shared control within limits. Is it true that most of us prefer to have an employer who treats us as capable of thinking for ourselves? Is it true great leaders provide a mission, a due date, some training, and then trust us to figure out the best way to achieve it? Providing enforceable statements and neutralizing student arguing are just two of the many ways the Love and Logic approach shares healthy amounts of thinking and control. We'll provide many additional ideas on this subject in chapter five.

Empathy

Without sincere empathy, there is no Love and Logic. Since free will exists among all of humanity, we cannot ensure that all educators set limits, avoid unwinnable arguments… or do anything else… in a way that demonstrates true caring and compassion. All we can accomplish is to emphasize the importance of doing so.

If you ever run into someone who complains, "I tried that Love and Logic, and it doesn't work," there's a good chance they are trying to apply it with anger, lectures, threats, coldness, or biting sarcasm.

Relationships

Healthy teacher-student relationships never happen without healthy limits set and enforced by the adult. Do challenging students truly bond with doormat-type teachers who try to be every kid's best friend? No way. They develop contempt for these adults, and spend most of their time manipulating and feeling out of control.

Do difficult students respect teachers who bark plenty of orders and issue threats that they can never enforce? Of course they don't.

As we keep emphasizing, students connect with educators who are able to establish themselves as being powerful and warm at the same time.

Limits set with enforceable statements and enforced with empathy are just part of the formula for establishing this power-warmth (or strong-loving) balance. We briefly introduced another approach in chapter one. You may recall that a young teacher, Lynne, was having quite a time with her rather rambunctious and defiant student, Philip. Her mentor suggested she work on their relationship by systematically noticing unique and special things about him. Let's look at the steps for applying this technique over a three-week experimental period:

The One-Sentence Intervention

STEP ONE: Identify six unique and positive things the student values.

These should be things valued by the student... not positive aspects of their behavior or attitude that you are hoping to reinforce. As we clarified in chapter one, the one-sentence intervention is not the "catch-them-when-they-are-good" technique. Instead, it represents a genuine attempt by the adult to value the student for who they are... the wonderful parts and the warts as well.

We come to respect, admire, and model after those who value us unconditionally.

This doesn't mean valuing all behavior unconditionally.

This means valuing each student regardless of how negative their behavior might be.

Many teachers describe how difficult it can be to identify six unique and positive things that their hard-to-love students value. One helpful strategy involves having all of our students complete an interest inventory at the beginning of the year. This can give us some clues as to what they're into and what they value.

Perhaps many of us simply make this harder than it has to be, thinking we need to notice big and important things. Oftentimes noticing the smallest, even rather mundane things seems to have an even bigger impact. For example, the student...

- likes to draw.
- likes to wear boots.
- doesn't let anyone push him around.
- has a scrape or other "wound."
- likes a certain type of shoe.
- has shoes (for the little ones).
- plays a certain sport.

- is loyal to friends.
- rides a bike to school.
- drives to school.
- likes a certain type of music.
- plays an instrument.
- likes to wear shoes without socks.
- likes animals.
- has a pet. (This is a big one!)

STEP TWO: Write each of these six unique things in the format, "I noticed that_____. I noticed that."

Don't end the statement with "and that's great." Simply end it with "I noticed." Challenging students frequently react negatively to praise. It's as if they think, *I'm not that great. What's this person want from me? What's their agenda? I better show them that buttering me up is not going to work!*

STEP THREE: Share with the student two of these statements per week for three weeks.

Do this when they are calm, and do this when it will not embarrass them around their peers. Seeing them in the hall, whisper, "I noticed that_____. I noticed that." Walking by their desk, whisper, "I noticed that_____. I noticed that."

If the student wants to talk about what you've shared, spend a few moments conversing. If they look uncomfortable or say something snide like, "So… you are so weird," just move away. You might even reply, "Yes. I noticed that, too."

During this time we are planting seeds. As good farmers, we know seeds don't sprout immediately. It takes some time and nurturing.

STEP FOUR: After three weeks, test your progress.

When the student is doing something you want them to stop… or is not doing something you'd like them to start, walk over and whisper, "Will you _____, just for me? Thanks." As the word "thanks" is coming out of your mouth, begin moving away from the student at a moderate rate of speed.

If they grumble, complain, or claim they aren't going to comply, just keep moving. Go back to teaching or whatever you were doing before you approached them.

By moving away, and by ignoring their grumbling, we send a powerful message: "I believe in you, and I know you will do this for me without a fight." In contrast, when we make the mistake of standing near them or hoping that the evil eye will do the trick, we send a far less positive expectation: "I just know you aren't going to comply. That's why I'll need to keep an eye on you and make you do what I want."

Kids either live up to… or down to… our expectations. Besides, it's always significantly less likely that we'll get pulled into an unwinnable power struggle when we are no longer there.

Kids either live up to… or down to… our expectations.

A teacher in one of my (Charles's) conferences kept complaining, "This won't work with my kids. This won't work with my kids."

Finally I asked her, "Tell me more. What are your kids like?"

She replied, "I teach high school special ed. I've got a self-contained classroom of some of the most difficult streetwise students you'll ever meet."

"I bet that's tough," I agreed. "How about if I make you a bet?"

She smiled, and replied, "I'm not typically the gambling type, but you are on!"

"Okay, here's the deal," I continued. "Use this on your toughest student. If they aren't willing to do something for you after sharing your 'I noticed' statements twice a week for three weeks, I'll send you one hundred dollars' worth of products from our Love and Logic catalog."

A month later I received a call. On the line was this very same teacher. She complained, "I'm so disappointed with that one-sentence intervention technique."

At a loss for words, I simply asked, "Didn't work?"

"Well, you see," she continued, "I used it with two of my students. I kept noticing little things about them just the way you explained. Three weeks went by, and I saw my opportunity to test it and get my two hundred bucks' worth of stuff. The two of them were sitting at a table together goofing around instead of working. I wandered over and whispered to both of them, 'Guys, will you get to work, just for me? Thanks.' Then I walked away. Behind my back I heard them mocking, 'Will you get to work just for me? Thanks.'"

I felt bad for her, and stated, "I'm so sorry this didn't work for you."

She answered, "No, I was elated. As I heard their nasty comeback, I thought to myself, 'That's two kids… that's two hundred bucks of stuff from Love and Logic!' What was so irritating is that when I had a chance to peek their way, they were fast at work."

I was confused. "Huh?"

She laughed. "I just called to tell you that it actually worked. I still can't believe it."

When teachers combine powerful limits, enforcement of these limits with empathy, and the one-sentence intervention, they dramatically stack the odds in favor of success with students. They also go a long way toward helping students whose emotional needs are not met at home.

Whenever we build a relationship with a student, we change their life. We don't always see the results, but scores of research tells us that it takes just one positive relationship to save a child.

Whenever we build a relationship, it also ups the odds that we'll end up truly liking the student. All of this goes both ways. We noticed something: Life is better when we truly like kids… particularly when we work with them on a daily basis!

CHAPTER FOUR

There's no Love or Logic without Sincere Empathy

Kurt had his priorities. School was rarely one of them. More important was keeping up on his texts, tweets, posts, voice messages... and of course... his video gaming acumen.

This year, Kurt was in a brand new grade with a brand new type of teacher, Mrs. Jacobson. His first English project, an essay showcasing the fine art of hyperbole, arrived on her desk later than a June bug in October. Kurt braced himself for the inevitable: Lectures about the importance of promptness and threats about the type of poor grade he'd receive if he didn't start completing assignments in a timelier manner. *Man*, he thought, *teachers and parents must be born with an extra part of the brain... the "lecture lobe."*

Did we mention that Mrs. Jacobson was different? Patting Kurt on the back, she replied with loving sadness, "Oh... Kurt... I can't imagine how upsetting it must have been to discover that this assignment was overdue."

Kurt, too confused to respond, grunted, "Uh..."

With sincere concern, Mrs. Jacobson continued, "The good news... Kurt... is that there will be some other assignments this year that you may be able to get credit for."

"You mean I'm getting a zero on that one?" Kurt inquired.

With empathy, she nodded, "Yes. Like I said, I can't imagine how disappointing this must be for you. Please let me know how I can help."

With awe and great sincerity, did Kurt smile and say, "Oh... Mrs. Jacobson... I am so thankful for this character-building experience. I just know that I am going to be a better man because of this. I bet this was hard for you, too. Can I give you a hug"?

The Reality

Wouldn't it be great if students actually reacted like that? Wouldn't it be amazing if there was some strategy for helping them see consequences as wonderful gifts intended to help them avoid a lifetime of pain and disappointment? Is this reality, or is it fantasy?

We've never seen a student respond like Kurt in the example above. Nevertheless, we have known numerous educators who've learned how to provide discipline without losing the admiration and respect of their students. Dr. Foster W. Cline and I (Jim) discovered the secret early in the evolution of Love and Logic.

The 1970s were an interesting time in America. Some kids were wearing bell-bottom pants. Even more were discovering that their parents and teachers couldn't tell them what to do. Up until this time, threats, lectures, and intimidation seemed to work with almost all youth. Yes, there was a time in America when adults could scare most kids into acting better. It still wasn't the best way to work with youth, but it *looked* like it worked.

As a child, my father (Jim's) employed a common approach termed "discipline with decibels." He'd yell, "Sit down, shut up, and listen!" My brothers and I would sit down, shut up, and listen. As the 1970s arrived, many kids changed their tune: "You can't talk to us that way! We're calling social services" or in response to teachers, "You talk to me that way, and my dad is gonna come down here and _____."

Against this societal backdrop, my friend Foster (Dr. Cline) and I began to develop the Love and Logic approach. Studying a wide array of research and theory in education and psychology, we became obsessed with the importance of two things:

Kids need limits.

In fact, kids crave... or yearn for... the very same limits they seem to protest the most.

Kids need to make plenty of affordable mistakes.

Children learn to make great decisions about big and important things by making plenty of mistakes over relatively small things *and* experiencing the relatively small natural or logical consequences.

Somehow, we thought, *we have to provide the boundaries and structure students need while at the very same time helping them learn to make respectful and responsible decisions.* The name **"Love and Logic"** was born:

Love

It takes a great amount of **Love** to set and enforce limits with kids. It also takes a large measure of **Love** to step back and allow them to make small mistakes.

Logic

The **Logic** is not something we provide from the outside with eloquent lectures or persuasive discourse. Instead, a valuable type of **Logic** develops within a child's heart and mind when they experience the consequences of their good and their poor decisions.

Foster and I were pretty proud of ourselves, and our heads became even bigger when parents and educators began to tout the effectiveness of what we were teaching in our classes:

Learning from Mistakes

Children learn from their mistakes when:

- they experience the consequences of their mistakes, and
- adults in their environment provide empathy.

Bad choices have natural consequences. If David fails to wear a coat, he gets cold. If Jan misses the school bus, she has to pay her mom for the trip to school.

Adults are tempted to scold and reprimand but may be surprised to learn that children actually learn best from consequences when adults empathize with them.

- "It's never fun to be cold, David."
- "I can't imagine how frustrating it was to see the bus pulling away without you."

When adults reprimand, children often transform sorrow over their choice into anger with the adult — and the lesson is lost.

When adults express sincere sorrow, children have a significant learning opportunity. David may think, *Tomorrow I'll wear my coat.* Jan may decide, *I'll get up fifteen minutes earlier tomorrow.*

Empathy + The Consequence = Learning

"Thanks so much, Jim and Foster. Things are better in my classroom and home! The kids are way more respectful and responsible."

Pride comes before the fall. Like a balloon in a cacti garden, our growing egos suddenly shriveled to a more appropriate size:

"Thanks for nothing, Jim and Foster. You ruined my classroom and my home! Now the kids are more resentful and rebellious."

We were dismayed. We kept pondering, *How is it that about half of the people are so successful with these concepts... and about half are not?*

Shoplifting

About that time two local fourteen-year-old girls, Beth and Sarah, walked into the local drug store, hoping to acquire a "five-finger-discount" on cosmetics: Being busted for shoplifting was the result.

At that time, Evergreen, Colorado was a small and tightknit community. As such, both sets of parents had taken the parenting course Foster and I taught. Getting together to commiserate and plan, both sets decided to address the problem in the same way. Their thinking was, *If they both have the same consequences, they won't be able to play us against each other.*

As their plan ran its course, Beth proclaimed to everyone in the community who'd listen, "My parents are so pathetic. I can't believe what they did! I wouldn't have all of these problems if they weren't so uptight and clueless. I can't wait to get out of their #$%@$# house."

> *People excuse all sorts of inappropriate behavior*
> *by blaming those around them.*

Sarah's response was very different. "Mr. Fay," she said with downcast eyes, "I can't believe I did that. That was so stupid."

I (Jim) responded, "So I hear that your parents and Beth's are making you guys do even more community service than the judge ordered. I bet that makes you really mad."

Her response was shocking: "Yeah... well... I guess not really. They just want me to have a good life... and... like they love me and don't want me to go to prison someday."

Empathy expressed by the adult drives the pain
of the consequence deep into the heart where it can grow
into character and wisdom.

Off I went to tell Dr. Cline, my buddy and renowned psychiatrist. "Foster," I said, "you know so-and-so who got arrested at the drug store for stealing makeup?"

"Which so-and-so?" he inquired.

"Sarah," I replied. "You won't believe this. She just told me... more or less... that what she did was stupid and that her parents did what they did because they love her."

"What?" Foster answered. "That's a far cry from what Beth is spouting around town!"

"Yes," I agreed, "both of their parents seemed to use what we teach... but why the big difference in how their kids reacted? I've known both of them since they were little girls. Both of the kids have about the same personality. I mean... I could understand it if one was born a lot more strong-willed than the other... but... well that just doesn't seem to be the case."

Foster studied the floor, scratched his head, and replied with a wry grin, "You know, Jim, I don't think they taught us that in psychiatry school."

My mouth hung open.

Foster continued, "Think about it, Jim. If we could figure this out and share it with the world, what a gift it would be. What if we could teach people how to discipline kids without losing their love and respect? That would be amazing!"

This discussion launched the two of us on a passionate journey of discovery. Answers didn't come from books, research journal articles, university courses, seminars, or reexamination of the educational and psychological theories. They came from observations and interviews with highly effective educators and topnotch parents. It was all Foster's idea. "Hey, Jim," he suggested, "let's study the folks who have success and compare what they do with those who don't."

It all started with comparing the way Beth and Sarah's parents handled the shoplifting saga. Both girls were expected to do extra community service. Both were required to complete extra chores at home to repay their parents for the time and energy drained as a result of their parents having to accompany them to court. Both were restricted for three months from visiting any stores without direct parental supervision.

Let's view how Beth's parents delivered the consequences:

"Beth, you know better than to do something like that! That makes us so mad. You look at us when we're talking to you! You know good and well what stealing does to your reputation, and we're not going to have any more of that nonsense. You're doing extra community service, and you're definitely going to pay us back for all of the time and energy we've had to put into this. Don't you roll your eyes! And... you can forget about going into any store without us being there. I hope this teaches you a lesson!"

Beth's reaction was predictable. "Oh, fine! Just fine! You guys don't understand anything. I hate you! You can #%&#%#," and with that she ran to her room slamming the door.

Let's consider how Sarah's parents delivered the very same consequences:

"Oh... Sarah. This is really sad. We can't even guess how awful you must feel about this. We imagine you must be feeling really scared."

Sarah stared at the floor.

Her parents continued, "What sorts of things can you do to go above and beyond what the judge has ordered? We mean... how can you show everyone how really sorry you are?"

Sarah replied, "I don't know."

"We bet it's really hard to think of things... especially when you are feeling as bad as you are. There's some good news. We aren't going to restrict you from shopping without us forever. Do you think six months would be about right?"

Sarah reacted, "That's way too long."

"Maybe you're right," they replied. "Would it be better if we made it only three months?"

"I guess so," a relieved Sarah answered. "Thanks."

Sincere Empathy Allows Their Problem to Remain Theirs

As people often say, "It's all in the delivery." Both parents loved their girls, and both were deeply devoted to helping them learn from their poor decision to shoplift. Both provided the same consequences. Only one set delivered this discipline in a way that allowed the problem to remain the child's problem.

Beth's parents immediately put her in fight or flight by raising their voices and lecturing. Neurologically speaking, the parts of her brain responsible for self-control, learning, and problem solving shut down. All she could think about was protecting herself by casting blame upon her parents.

With a sincere dose of empathy, *prior to describing the consequences,* Sarah's parents allowed the parts of her brain devoted to self-control, learning, and cause and effect to function at high levels. Because she was able to see that her parents cared for her and were understanding of her plight, she was forced to own her problem. Her parents were the "good guys"... which required her to see her bad decision as the "bad guy."

The effective teacher administers consequences with empathy and understanding instead of anger, lectures, or sarcasm.

I (Charles) watched the power of empathy being used on one of the founders of Love and Logic, my father, Jim. It all began when we decided to take an adult-only vacation together as a family. As a grownup, have you ever traveled with your parents? Fortunately, we've enjoyed a great relationship throughout the years, so the trip was a joy.

As we left their house, my mother turned to my father and asked politely, "Jim, do you really need to bring your laptop?"

With furrowed brow, he replied, "Well, I'm just going to do a little work."

She knew well enough to leave it alone. Much to her credit, she didn't say another word.

A week went by, and we had a wonderful time. Driving home from the airport, my father's eyes widened in horror, as he asked, "Shirley, did you grab my laptop?"

"No, honey, I never had it," she replied sweetly.

"You didn't?" he grumbled with obvious annoyance. "Why didn't you grab it?"

I was so proud of her response! With sincere loving kindness… without a hint of sarcasm… she empathized, "Oh, no… Jim… I can't imagine how upsetting that must be."

In response to her loving reply, I saw a man of over seventy years become nine, when he said, "Well… you don't have to rub it in!"

Some questions for you:

- Did my mother "rub it in," or was it her sincere empathy that allowed my dad to experience the full brunt of his poor decision?
- Has anyone ever made you really mad… in the short term… by being really kind and caring?
- Is it true that empathy forces us to face our poor decision rather than finding it easy to blame the person providing it?
- Do any of us truly like to own the problems we create?
- Can we learn from our problems if we never own them?

While upset in the short term, my father soon realized that there was a good reason he'd married my mother back in 1956. "I'm sorry, Shirley," he admitted a couple miles later, "I guess I really blew it."

She remained a class act! "That's okay, Jim. I'm sure that happens to a lot of people."

Anger or Sarcasm Makes Their Problem Ours

In a strange way, it's almost easier for us when people are nasty. We find it easier to blame them for our misdeeds. If my mom had replied with sarcasm, "Well, Jim, why'd you have to bring that laptop in the first place?" would he have been off the hook… and she on it?

Do you want your students to blame you for their poor decisions? Or is it far better for everyone involved that they carry this weight?

Examples, Examples, Examples

Love and Logic is famous for offering practical techniques… and plenty of examples, which help us learn. Examples help us see how we might apply tools in our unique life situation.

SUSPENDED FOR FIGHTING

Marcus has been waiting in the outer office for his appointment with Mr. Bukowski, one of the assistant principals at his high school. He's about to receive a three-day suspension for instigating a fistfight in the cafeteria.

Is Mr. B. a Love and Logic guy? Let's find out.

"Okay, Marcus," says Mr. Bukowski, "you know the rule about fighting here on campus.

> **How to Destroy the Teaching Value of A Logical Consequence**
>
> - Say, "This will teach you a lesson."
> - Display anger or disgust.
> - Explain the value of the consequence.
> - Moralize or threaten.
> - Talk too much.
> - Feel sorry and "give in."
> - Contrive a consequence for the purpose of "getting even."

You've read the student conduct policy. You've signed it. Your dad signed it as well. You know we don't put up with that kind of blatant disregard for the rules, and you knew before you did it that it would earn you a three-day suspension, but you did it anyway. I don't want to see you on campus for the next three days."

Marcus retorts, "But you don't understand. It's not my fault. That kid's always in my face and my dad says I don't have to put up with it. Besides, you guys never do anything to him. How come it's always me, huh? This sucks!"

"I don't want to hear it. You know the rules. You're excused."

There's no sincere empathy here. Where there's no empathy there is no Love and Logic.

The odds are high that we can accurately predict what Marcus does next. What happens to the door as he leaves? What happens to the kids who are unlucky enough to be in his way as he exits the school? What happens to the lockers as he goes down the hall? What happens with spray paint outside of the school that night? Whom does Marcus see as the problem? Is it his bad decision or Mr. Bukowski's?

Compare this scenario with a different assistant principal, Mr. Katz, dealing with the same scenario:

"Wow… Marcus… this is so unfortunate. That kid must have really gotten under your skin. Man… I can only wonder if you found yourself in a jam, thinking, 'If I fight him it's a three-day suspension, and if I don't, he's going to keep it up and nobody around here will respect me.' So… what are we looking at here? Just because I care about you, do you think I can stand in the way of the consequences?"

"Well, I guess not," Marcus replied. "I guess I'm suspended… but it's not fair."

"I bet you're worried that Jeff is off the hook," said Mr. Katz.

"Well…"

"Not to worry, Marcus," the principal empathized, "he's on the hook for three days as well. We'll look forward to seeing both of you on Monday. Let me know if you need some help thinking of other ways to keep him off your back."

Mr. Katz understands the power of sincere empathy. As a result, is Marcus more likely to be angry... or more likely to be confused?

One principal's actions brought out the worst in a student. Another's brought out the best. What was the secret to the second one's success? He preceded the consequence with sincere understanding and empathy, instead of anger, lectures, threats, or sarcasm.

Provide a strong and sincere dose of empathy
before delivering the consequences.

That's Love and Logic!

LATE ASSIGNMENT

Teacher A:

"Wow, a late assignment. This has to be really disappointing after all your hard work. Even though I can't give you credit toward your grade, I'd be glad to read it and let you know how you did. Is there anything I can do to help you avoid this kind of problem in the future?"

Teacher B:

"I can't accept this assignment. You've missed the deadline. If you want to get credit for these assignments you are going to have to turn them in on time."

Which teacher *really* used Love and Logic?

ENTERING THE CLASSROOM WITH AN ATTITUDE

Teacher A:

"You need to settle down. I don't want you in here with that attitude."

Teacher B:

"Oh, no. It looks like you're having a rough day. Is there any way I can help?"

Which teacher is seen as the enemy? Which is more likely to be seen as an ally?

> **LOVE AND LOGIC EXPERIMENT:**
> ## Do We Have To Do This?
>
> STUDENT: "Do we have to do this assignment?"
>
> TEACHER: "Only if you want credit for it."

DRUGS IN YOUR LOCKER

Principal A says:

"The school resource officer found drugs in your locker. That's against district rules and that's against the law. You are suspended for the rest of the year, and I'm sure you'll need to go to court and explain it to the judge."

Principal B says:

"Ohhhh… this is unfortunate. Drugs were found in your locker. No matter how much we care for you, we can't stand between these facts and what the district policy says. The sad news is that this brings with it a full year suspension… and you may have to visit with a judge."

> *A mistake can be a great teacher,*
> *provided the student is allowed to experience*
> *the consequences of the mistake.*

CELL PHONE DISTRACTION

Teacher A frowns, then says:

"You need to put that cell phone away now. That's distracting."

Teacher B says with a smile:

"It must be great to be so popular. I can understand wanting to text right now. Can you put that away so it doesn't remain a distraction, or would it be better for you to give it to me until the end of class? You decide."

HASSLING EACH OTHER ON THE PLAYGROUND

Playground Monitor A whispers:
"It looks like you guys are really having a hard time. That happens to a lot of people. I don't want to see you get into trouble. There's a seat over there on the bench. We'll try it again tomorrow."

Playground Monitor B quips with sarcasm:
"Well… I guess it's just too hard for you guys to get along. Go sit on the bench and we'll see if you can make better choices tomorrow."

LOVE AND LOGIC EXPERIMENT:
Playground Problems

STUDENT: (Other kids have been complaining that he causes problems on the playground. Teacher does not know what to believe, but tends to believe the complainers.)

TEACHER: "Jason, we are going to conduct a diagnostic experiment. That's where we diagnose the problem. I'm going to keep you off the playground for five days. If the problem stops, what do you think I'll think? If the problem continues even without you being on the playground, what do you think I'll think?"

STUDENT: "But it's not fair."

TEACHER: "It's not punishment. It's an experiment."

STUDENT: "But it's not fair."

TEACHER (with sincere empathy): "I bet it feels that way. Hang in there."

LATE TO SCHOOL

With genuine concern, Teacher A says:

"I was worried about you. I'm so glad you made it. Please let me know if there is anything I can do to help."

Lecturing, Teacher B says:

"Why can't you get here on time?"

UNAUTHORIZED URL

Teacher A says:

"Videogaming.com is not on the list of URLs you can use in class. You knew that already. You're not using the computer until I know that I can trust you, and you're going to have to use books to complete this assignment instead!"

Teacher B says:

"Ohhhh… bummer… that website, videogaming.com, is not on the list of URLs for use in class. Even sadder is I'm not feeling that I can trust you to use the computer right now. There are some ways you can get this assignment accomplished by the end of the period without going online. Please let me know if you would like to hear about them."

Learning from consequences is a struggle that can cause pain. Surviving this struggle is a great self-concept builder.

Empathy Doesn't Always Come Naturally

If we were new to Love and Logic and reading this chapter we'd probably be thinking, *Yeah, right! This looks good on paper, but how do you make it work with real kids in the real world?*

We might even be like the parent in South Carolina who blurted out during one of our trainings: "Ain't natural! Ain't natural to be so nice to a young'un when they just done something that makes you so mad. I'll tell you what I say. 'I brought you into this world and I can take you right out. When Momma ain't happy ain't nobody gonna be happy!'"

While rather coarse in her delivery, her response rings with truth. It's not natural for most people to remain empathetic when a student has just acted out. Many of us tend to default to an angry, frustrated, threatening, sarcastic response. We do so for three primary reasons.

First, many of us were raised by good parents and educated by good teachers who typically responded to misbehavior with anger, lectures, or threats. As such, we witnessed this behavior thousands and thousands of times by the time we became adults. As a result, it became deeply embedded in our subconscious minds and serves as our "go-to" when kids make poor decisions or misbehave. In the marrow of our bones, we find ourselves believing that we must get angry, lecture, or issue threats so kids will understand the seriousness of their misdeeds.

The second reason has to do with "mirror neurons." Brain research has documented the existence of specific neurons that help us understand and actually experience… "mirror"… the emotions of those around us. We've all experienced these neurons in action. How do we feel when we're around someone who's sad… or angry… or negative… or anxious… or even positive? The answer is obvious. We find the emotions of others rubbing off on us.

Ironically, these wonderful neurons that help us empathize with the feelings of others also make it more difficult for us to empathize with angry, negative, or sarcastic students. Their negativity often infects us. Daily, we must ask ourselves two questions:

Who's rubbing off on whom?

Are the emotions of my students infecting me, or is my calmness, enthusiasm, and empathy inspiring them?

The third reason empathy can be so difficult is that student misbehavior can be really annoying. It's that simple. Sometimes students do really irritating things. It doesn't mean that we don't love our students. We can love people and at the same time find their behavior extremely taxing.

Sometimes it's helpful to give yourself permission to say… only to yourself… "I'm really having a challenging time liking this kid."

It's okay to be human. Ironically, when we accept our own feelings, it often enhances our ability to realize something essential: The students we find the most difficult to like are those who need our empathy the most.

Time and time again, we've heard teachers admit:

"I realized that I wasn't the only one having difficulty liking this student. This led me toward feeling genuine sadness for him. In turn, I began to see him as a hurting person rather than one intentionally bent on making my professional life miserable."

Making Empathy More Natural

We've had people come to us in tears, saying:

"I'm so relieved to know I don't have to get angry when my kids do something wrong. I was raised to believe that you have to get stern and angry when kids misbehave. I grew up seeing my teachers do this, too."

"Wow! What a difference it makes using empathy, instead."

"My problem is that… too frequently… anger or sarcasm comes out of my mouth instead. I just can't seem to do the empathy consistently."

Often hearing this feedback, Dr. Cline and I (Jim) changed our teacher training courses in the 1980s. We emphasized the importance of empathy and the fact that our empathy must come *before* we deliver consequences... not after. The educators in our classes were also learning to use "brief empathetic statements," and they were encouraged to use just one that fit their personality or culture. These included:

- How sad...
- Oh, man...
- This is so sad...
- Oh... this must be upsetting...
- What a bummer...

This was helping. The educators we trained were experiencing more success demonstrating sincere empathy, but we were still hearing some lament, "My empathetic statement sort of feels phony sometimes," or "I still can't remember what to say when the heat is on." A few were even complaining, "It sounds good in theory. It just doesn't work in real life."

In the face of this apparent setback, we were still witnessing the great success enjoyed by thousands and thousands of Love and Logic educators and parents. We wondered, "What's missing in our understanding of empathy? What can we do to help people more consistently provide it in sincere ways?" We decided to continue our observations of the most highly successful people.

I (Jim) observed a wise parent in West Virginia listening to her kids as they came home from school. "Mom," one of them yelled, "that stupid bus driver gave us assigned seats and now we can't sit with our friends!"

"Ohhhhhhh," she empathized in a truly sincere way.

"Yeah, and we didn't get to go out to recess because we forgot to do our homework!"

"Ohhhhhh. Give me a hug."

I was quick to ask, "Do you just make that sound, 'Ohhhhhh' every time? Is that how you demonstrate empathy every time your kids have a problem?"

"Sure do," she replied. "I suppose I use it with my husband, too."

Now I had a chance to do some real, professional in-depth research. "Why?" I inquired.

"Well," she said, "if I had to think even for a split second about what to say, I'd already be into my angry mood. So, Jim, I just keep that on the tip of my tongue so I don't say stuff I'd be sorry for later."

Then she added, "My daddy taught me that if I make a sound like that it changes how I feel right away. When I use that sound, I start to see how my kids are feeling… rather than being so mad."

Still, not being as smart as her daddy, I asked, "Well, isn't it redundant to say the same thing every time?"

"Well," she reflected, "my daddy used to say that people are starved for having others understand how they feel, and they don't care how it sounds when they try to do it. They're just relieved."

Using an Empathetic Sound

This wise country lady helped us solve the mystery about why it was so difficult for some of our class participants to adopt the empathy-then-consequence formula. From that day on we began to experiment with offering the option of providing an empathetic *sound* rather than statement. Of course, we suggest choosing one that feels comfortable, calms you down, and comes across as sincere. For many, success with empathy comes when they keep this sound on the tip of the tongue. This way, it comes out of their mouths before anything else.

Using Delayed Consequences

"Dr. Fay," she called out during the conference, "what do you do when a student has just done something awful… something that leaves you feeling psycho?"

I asked her to clarify. "So… can you give me an example?"

"She called me 'fatso,'" she answered. "It wouldn't have made me so mad if I hadn't felt so self-conscious about my weight since junior high. I just wanted to strangle her… I mean… of course I didn't… but the thought was more than fleeting."

I appreciated her honesty.

Is it true that some students search for our deepest insecurities and hit these wounds with poison darts? How do we provide empathy when a student has just placed themselves on our last nerve?

I replied, "So… the good news is that you didn't strangle the kid. What'd you do instead?"

She answered, "All I could think to say was, 'I handle things when I'm calm. We'll talk about this later.'"

Are there times when it's simply impossible, and even unwise, to provide an immediate dose of empathy? Are there times when the smartest thing we can do is delay the consequences?

"That sounds good. How did she react?" I inquired.

"She acted like she didn't care," she answered, "but I could see she was irritated that I wasn't trying to deal with the problem right then."

When we delay consequences, does it give us time to calm down and reflect on the appropriate course of action? Does it allow us to consider how we might provide sincere empathy as we firmly hold the student accountable for the problem they created?

By the way, what happened with this student? After the conference, this teacher described her intervention:

"I decided to go to her later that week and say, 'I can't even imagine how bad you must feel about yourself to say something like that. I'm really feeling for you.' She tried to act all

tough, but I could see that I hit a nerve. Now she is doing a lot of 'community service' at the school and even at home. Anytime there's a job to be done, she's our go-to. I'm not sure it will change her, but I think it's been more effective than clutching her around the throat and squeezing. As a teacher, that never looks good on your résumé."

Empathy Helps Us Stay Sane

In a broader sense, how does using empathy help us navigate our challenging world with less stress? It allows us to experience, truly feel, the fact that we must allow others to shoulder their problems. We begin to realize that it is not our job… and not even within our ability… to make others have happy and responsible lives.

Our role is to take good care of ourselves in caring, unselfish ways while allowing others to learn from the consequences of their poor decisions.

Isn't it freeing to see that you can remain the "good guy" while allowing others' poor decisions to remain the "bad guy"?

Remember...

When you don't know what to do… or you're too angry to think straight, delay the consequence. "I'm going to have to do something about this."

CHAPTER FIVE

Gaining Control by Sharing It

The presentation was over, and here she came. "Jim, that was a good presentation, but now I've got to go home and apologize to my husband. I've been calling him a wimp. I've told him a dozen times to have a little backbone when it comes to our kids, but he never listens."

"Wow. Tell me about that," I responded.

"Well, I just always assumed they behaved better for him than they do for me because he's a man. Now I know it has nothing to do with that."

Creating a "Savings Account" of Control

"He hardly ever lays down the law to them. He's constantly giving them choices. But now that I heard your presentation I realize what he's been doing. He's a master of what you just taught the group. You called it the savings account approach to control."

"That's right," I answered her. "It's all about making little deposits in the form of small choices so that we can make withdrawals when we really need to tell kids what to do."

She nodded, and said, "Yes... and now that I think about it, I see him doing it all the time. He's constantly making little deposits, giving them tiny choices about things he doesn't care about. Then when he has to boss them around he makes a withdrawal from that account. I saw him doing this last night with the kids during their bedtime."

She continued with a description of her husband's wonderful mastery of Love and Logic:

> "Hey, guys. It's bedroom time." Then he asked, "Do you want to walk to the bedroom on your own or have piggyback rides tonight?"
>
> "Piggyback rides!" they replied.
>
> "Great! Here we go."
>
> Once they were in their room, he gave another choice. "Do you want a story or no story?"
>
> "Story, Daddy, story!"
>
> After the story, the deposits continued: "Do you want the light on or light off? Music on or music off? Covers on or covers off? Will you be sleeping with your heads at the top of the bed or the bottom? You decide. Kisses or no kisses?"
>
> Preparing to leave the room, he said, "I love you guys… see you in the morning."

Taking Withdrawals from the Account

Like all wonderful young children, they began to whine, "But, Daddy, we don't want you to go. We want to be with you and Mommy."

Because of the small deposits he'd repeatedly made, his account was well funded. Now he was poised to take a withdrawal. "Wait a minute, guys. Who has been making all the decisions here tonight? You have. Now it's my turn. Thanks for understanding. I love you. Goodnight."

As "goodnight" rolled off his tongue, he exited their room.

Make deposits with tiny choices. Save the big decisions for yourself.

The woman continued, "Jim, until you taught us about creating a savings account of control, I had no idea what he was doing. Now I realize he never gives them choices about issues that affect us. He's letting them make decisions about things that only affect them, and each choice they make is one more deposit into his control account."

We either give kids control on our terms, or they take it on their terms.

In this situation, Dad gave away the control he didn't need. There was no need for him to control how his kids went to their room, whether they had the light on or off, whether or not they listened to music, or whether they slept on top or under their blankets. These issues only affected the kids.

Notice that he didn't even try to control whether or not they went to sleep. This is something he had no control over in the first place. If that's true, why not give it away as well. The only control Dad needed was for the kids to go to bed, and that was the only demand he made.

Dealing with Power Struggles

Power is a major issue between children and adults. While still very young, some kids realize they don't have much control over anything. A toddler unconsciously thinks, *I'm the smallest. They tell me what to do, and I don't get to make decisions. I need to find a way to get some control.* Then, winning the power struggle becomes all important — more than making good decisions.

When we offer kids a choice instead of making a demand, no power struggle ever begins. When we make a demand, we own the wise choice, leaving the child with only one way to win the power struggle — by making a foolish choice. Given a range of choices, a child has endless opportunities to choose wisely.

*The more control we give away, the easier it is to
take control when it becomes necessary.*

Compare this dad's method with a similar bedtime situation
in which the father tries to take one hundred percent of the
control. The children are left feeling that they have practically
none: "Okay, kids. It's time to go to bed. Let's do it now."

*When people feel a loss of control they will do
whatever it takes to get it back.*

ARGUING

"But, Dad, it's too early. We're not tired. Why do we have to go
to bed when we're not tired? Our friends don't have to go to bed
this early! You're treating us like babies!"

PASSIVE RESISTANCE

They make it look as if they are being cooperative, but they drag
their feet. All activity goes into slow motion.

PASSIVE AGGRESSION

They suddenly remember that the teacher told them to have
their parents test them on their spelling words. They have
personal issues that need to be discussed before they can go to
sleep. After their door is shut, they need water, the bathroom,
attention to nagging pains, etc. They may even wet their beds.
They complain about room temperature, strange noises, sibling
behaviors, etc. On a subconscious level, all of this is done to
make the parents "pay" for demanding control.

OUTRIGHT DEFIANCE

They refuse to stay in their bedroom, making constant trips to
their parents' bed. The fighting required to get them back into

their rooms is horrendous. When they become older children and teens, they may even sneak out at night.

Much of this resistant, even aggressive behavior is done on an automatic and subconscious level, and it serves to communicate: "Okay, Dad. You can try to make us do it, but you can't make us do it your way! Now who's in control?"

Control is like love.

The more control we give away, the more we get back.

The more control we try to take, the more we lose.

The Classroom: Sharing Control Within Limits

I (Jim) had visited her classroom several times and now my question to Mrs. Porter was, "Why do these kids work harder for you than they do for the other teachers?"

"I'm not sure," she replied, "but I think it's because I give them a lot more choices. I'll show you what I mean."

She began her lesson by passing out a sheet of math problems. Right away the kids groaned. "Twenty problems? That's too many. Why do we have to do so many?"

"Oh," she answered, "you only have to do half of them today. And since you're only going to do half, why don't you decide whether you want to do the odd numbered ones or the even numbered ones?"

I watched those kids so busy trying to decide between the odd and even ones that they seemed to have forgotten they didn't want to do any in the first place.

As Mrs. Porter passed by me she whispered, "I always give them twice as many as I want them to do. It gives them a chance to satisfy their control needs."

Her students had no more than finished that assignment when she passed out another sheet with twenty problems. "Oh, no," they complained. "We already did one set of problems. This is too much."

"Not to worry," she responded, "you don't have to do all of these either. I think only doing nine problems would be enough to show me that you've learned this. And as long as you are only doing nine… and you've already worked so hard… just pick out the nine easiest ones."

Now the kids were busy arguing with each other about whether multiplying by four was easier than multiplying by seven. They had already forgotten that they didn't want to do any of them.

"Isn't that great?" she whispered to me. "It probably takes more thinking for them to figure out which ones are easiest than it does to do all of the problems. You scc," she said, "I'm not looking for blind obedience. What I need from these kids is cooperation. Before I learned how to share control in this way I used to burn up a lot of my time and energy trying to get control. The more I fought for control, the more the kids resisted. I used to go home each night exhausted and disappointed."

She added, "I also have an easy way to find out which concepts the kids need help with. Periodically I give them the choice to leave out two of the problems that are the most difficult. They're satisfying their subconscious control needs, and I don't need to spend a lot of time on a formal evaluation to get the same information. It saves time and I can react to their instructional needs a lot faster."

Mrs. Porter's strategic use of small choices intrigued me. So much so that I decided to talk with several of her students, selecting those notorious for disliking school. "Hey, guys," I asked, "tell me about Mrs. Porter. You seem to like her. Why is that?"

"She's pretty cool," they agreed. "She doesn't yell at us and she's not bossy like some of the other teachers. And she lets us decide a lot of things. It's like she knows how hard it is to be a kid."

Jerome interjected, "She even lets us pick one homework assignment every week that we can refuse to do. We get to have an 'A' on that one."

Maya interrupted, "Yeah... I've never had a teacher that did that! I try to figure out which one is going to be the most challenging. Sometimes I don't guess right, but that's cool. I think she might know I'm doing that 'cause she usually comes and asks me if I need help."

When I asked Mrs. Porter about letting them refuse to do one homework assignment each week, she laughed and said, "Oh, yeah. It's true. What they don't know is that I give one more assignment each week than I used to. It's like the retail stores that raise their prices and then advertise big discounts. I just figured if adults fall for that trick, kids would fall for it as well."

> ### *Teachers gain the cooperation they need when they give away the control they don't need.*

As a young parent, I (Charles) experienced something that made me cringe. There we were sitting on a park bench watching our three-year-olds play. Marc was ours, and... we'll call her Jessie... belonged to some dear friends. We loved spending time with them.... not their child... but them.

Jessie ran the home. As such, she also attempted to run the park, the grocery store, the library, various restaurants, and any other places she visited. As we sat, watching her fine-tune her fascist techniques with other unsuspecting children, her father turned to me and asked, "Have you seen the movie Titanic with Leonardo DiCaprio?"

I replied, "Yeah. I saw it. It was pretty good."

Jessie's mother piped up, "Do you think it would be appropriate for a three-year-old?"

I thought she was joking, as I replied, "Well... let's see... there's extreme terror, some violence, lots of death... even a rather graphic suicide... I guess it would pass." (Please know I was being sarcastic.)

Dad was disappointed. "Oh... I guess we'll stay home."

I agreed, "I wouldn't recommend taking Jessie, but why don't you guys leave her with us sometime and have a date night?"

As these words came out of my mouth, I said to myself, *What were you thinking? They might actually take us up on the offer!*

More or less in unison, Mom and Dad answered, "Oh… we couldn't do that. We asked her if it would be okay for us to do that, but she said 'no.'"

Ouch! It was at that precise moment that my opinion was solidified: The concept of allowing children to make choices may be the most dramatically misunderstood concept in all of education and psychology.

Guidelines for Sharing Control *Within Limits*

Love and Logic is not a democracy. Our students… or our kids at home… don't get to vote on everything we do. Love and Logic is more like a benevolent monarchy. We as parents and educators have the ultimate say. Because kids need the safety of having caring authority figures, we don't hesitate to view ourselves as wise and kind kings or queens.

Because we want children to enjoy plenty of opportunities to make decisions and experience the positive and negative consequences, we "gift" them many small opportunities to do so. Because we know we gain control by sharing it, we "gift" bits and pieces of it so that we gain more cooperation.

The key is remembering that the Love and Logic approach *does not* advocate giving choices. It advocates giving *choices within limits*. That's why we provide the following guidelines for providing them:

> ### *For each choice, offer two options, each of which will make you happy.*

Jessie's parents offered one option that would make them happy: "You may stay with a sitter while Mommy and Daddy have a date," and another that wouldn't: "We will stay home with you instead."

When we make this mistake, we shouldn't be surprised when the child chooses the option we don't like.

Many teachers have found it easier to come up with effective choices when they have some examples. The following list was created by a group of educators attending one of our conferences. These are merely examples. Use some if they fit, or create some of your own. Most importantly, remember that each option you provide should leave you happy.

Feel free to...
-put your desks in a circle or in rows.
-whisper or talk quietly.
-choose your own partner or have the teacher choose your partner.
-edit your assignment or have a partner do it.
-have lights on or off.
-have music on or off.
-type this assignment or write it neatly.
-write in print or cursive.
-use black ink or blue.
-turn in your homework at the beginning of class or at the end.
-use crayons or colored pencils.
-choose topic one, two, or three for your written assignment.
-read your book on the floor or in your seat.
-do your assignment standing or seated.
-play a group game or an individual game.
-do the assignment by acting it out, reading, or writing it.
-pick one homework assignment to refuse to do and still get credit for it.
-choose the order in which to do the lesson.
-choose a topic to study from several listed on the board.
-pass your papers forward or backward.
-have homework Monday through Wednesday or Wednesday through Friday.
-take the test on Friday or Monday.
-get your current events assignment from a newspaper, magazine, or the internet.
-go to the computer lab with the Monday group or the Friday group.
-turn your work in on time for full credit, or later for a lower grade.

PROVIDE CHOICES WITHIN LIMITS PRIMARILY AS A PREVENTATIVE MEASURE

Most adults find it difficult to provide effective choices in the face of a disruption. During these times, our brains tend to go into fight or flight. As such, the only choices that come to mind are threats: "Settle down or go to the principal's office!"

Thinking of choices usually requires a calm mind. For a teacher, that is usually when he is experiencing a high level of cooperation. This is the time to make deposits into the account.

I (Jim) met a teacher who provided a unique choice. On his desk were two wire baskets. The label on one said, "Papers to be graded this week." The label on the other read, "Papers to be graded during the summer."

Upon seeing these baskets, his twelfth graders asked, "But if we put papers in that other basket, how are we supposed to get our grades in time to graduate?"

Having learned a great deal from teens, he smiled, shrugged his shoulders, and mumbled, "I dunno." Then he added, "I kind of hope that the summer one will fill up."

"What?! That's nuts," a perplexed student blurted.

"You see," the teacher added, "I always miss students so much when they graduate. If that basket fills up, then I get to have a whole extra year with them."

Even his students found a little humor in this one. One even laughed, and said, "We think you're okay, but not *that okay!*"

PROVIDE CHOICES BEFORE RESISTANCE NOT AFTER

Consider the following scenario involving Zack, a consistently defiant student. As you do, ask yourself, "Is this teacher really using Love and Logic?"

"Zack," said Mr. Jamison from across the room, "I'd like you to partner up with Jerome on this project."

As usual, Zack blurted, "No way, man! I'm not working with that dork. He messes up everything. Besides that, it's a stupid assignment in the first place."

With his authority being challenged in front of the class, Mr. Jamison decided to provide a choice. "Zack, would you rather work with Jenny or Phil?"

"No way, man. If I can't work with Tad, I'm not doing it at all, and you can dock my grade for all I care."

This situation has gone from bad to worse. Why?

First, Mr. Jamison gave Zack the stage by issuing a directive from across the room.

Secondly, is it possible that Zack's "control loss detector" triggered major defiance as soon as he was told what to do?

Thirdly, is there any chance that offering a choice *after* Zack became defiant emboldened his defiance? Might this be perceived by such a student as a sign of weakness?

> **When we provide choices after a student has become resistant, we reward their resistance.**

Consider how another teacher might handle this scenario.

Knowing that Zack looks for opportunities to "grandstand" in front of his classmates by arguing, Mrs. Lieberman casually leans over and whispers in Zack's ear, "Zack, would you rather work on this project with Sydney or Jimbo?"

"I'll do it with Tad."

Still whispering, she asks, "What were the choices, Zack?"

"I still want to do it with Tad."

"Zack," she responds calmly, "do I usually let you choose when I can?"

"I guess."

Preparing to move away quickly, she answers, "Well, this time I can't, so how about humoring me? I'll remember that you like to work with Tad. Thanks, pal."

Does Mrs. Lieberman's approach reduce the odds of chaos erupting? By providing a choice *before* the student became resistant, has she maintained her role as a powerful and caring authority figure? If he doesn't comply, can she delay the consequence and deal with the issue when it's convenient for her?

NEVER GIVE A CHILD A CHOICE THAT AFFECTS THE WELFARE OF ANOTHER PERSON

Jessie's parents, the couple who allowed their three-year-old to determine whether or not they went on a date without her, were the poster children for permissiveness. That's because they allowed their daughter to make major decisions that affected the welfare of others. One definition of permissiveness is allowing children to make decisions that affect the lives of others. No parent with an iota of common sense would allow their kids to make decisions about how the family money is spent. That decision affects others. In contrast, wise parents are quick to provide choices about how their children spend their own money. If the child makes a good choice, they learn. If they make a poor choice, they learn… without creating hardship for anyone else.

Err on the side of smaller choices rather than larger ones.

Because control is such a deep-seated emotional need, each choice, large or small, serves as a deposit into the account. A choice about juice or milk with breakfast is just as valued to the subconscious mind's drive for control as a choice of greater magnitude. A tiny choice about completing one worksheet first versus another is valued to the subconscious mind as a much larger one.

It's not the size of the choices we provide, it's the frequency with which we provide tiny ones.

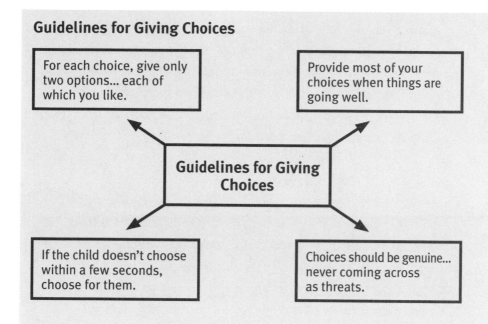

Because of this, we should never feel obligated to offer bigger choices potentially creating large problems down the road for ourselves or others.

Dave Funk describes how a mom, attempting to provide too broad of a choice, actually backed herself into a corner with her son.

Whenever I think of choices, I remember an incident that happened at a local restaurant. After an especially difficult day, I was comforting myself with some coffee and a piece of banana cream pie when I noticed two women and a little boy enter.

They were seated in a booth across the room from me, and I heard the mother say to the boy, "Pick out something to eat." I paid little attention beyond that point, other than to note they looked like a happy threesome.

Soon, the waitress came over, and I overheard her ask the boy what he wanted. As soon as the question was asked, he said, "Sketty." As soon as he said that, his mother said, "You are not getting spaghetti. You are getting a hot dog." What I saw next was a lesson in what happens when we provide too large of a choice... and then try to narrow the options.

The mother had first given the boy too broad of a choice for his age, suggesting that he "pick out something to eat." The boy complied. Then, the mother narrowed the limits to zero choices. Whether she was aware of this or not, she was saying, "Let the battle begin."

The first thing I noticed was the boy controlling the direction of the adult conversation. Before the battle, the two women had been engaged in pleasant talk. Now they were both looking at the kid. The second thing I saw was the kid controlling the color of his mother's face. It was interesting to see that change even through her heavy makeup.

I think the kid started to get high on this control, because he continued on the offensive and found that he was able to control the volume of his mother's voice and the number of words she produced: "Danny, quit that. Danny, eat your food. Danny, you just wait until we get home. You are going to get it, and I mean it!"

Then came the coup de grâce. I knew Danny had won when there was clear evidence that he had finally controlled his mother's very intellect. She said, "Danny, if you don't eat, I'm going to call the manager!"

I thought, Oh, yeah, lady. What are you going to say to the manager? My little boy is not eating, do something? *The mother lost a battle that never had to occur in the first place.*

To be given control and then have it taken away produces predictable results, whether with a kid at a restaurant, students in a school, or citizens of a country. Once we have it and lose it... we will fight to get it back.

IF THE STUDENT DOESN'T CHOOSE QUICKLY, CHOOSE FOR THEM

Standing in line for an unusual amount of time at a McDonald's restaurant, our friend Dr. Foster Cline assumed his new foster kids would have had plenty of time to decide what they would order. He was a younger parent and a younger psychiatrist. He was wrong.

They were racked with indecision. "Uh... I want a Happy Mmm... no, no... a big fries... but... no."

"I don't want hamburger... what are you gonna get?"

"I don't know... do they gots hotdogs? Where does it say hotdogs... I don't know..."

"Do they have root beer?"

Everyone in line behind them was fuming. So was Foster, our typically kind and patient buddy.

Finally another customer... one unencumbered by excess tact... yelled, "Good Lord. Order something for cryin' out loud. This is ridiculous!"

With that, Dr. Cline finally took charge. "I'm sorry," he said to everyone. Then he turned to the counter person, and said, "Cancel those orders. They'll have three salads and three waters."

These kids were madder than cats in a bathtub. They ate their meals with obvious attitudes and complained all the way home. Knowing that any explanations, lectures, or attempts to console would simply feed the fire, Foster didn't say a word.

The following week they once again stopped at the same McDonald's for an after-church meal. When it was their turn to order, the counter person had a different problem. "Hey, guys. Slow down. Why are you talking so fast? Let's take it one at a time."

The oldest of the three apologized, "Sorry, man. We got this new foster dad, and if we don't order fast, he gets us nasty stuff."

Dr. Cline learned an important lesson about providing choices: We do it on our terms not our kids' terms.

We give choices on our terms... not on the kids' terms.

Mr. Gustafson, a much loved teacher in our area, made it a yearly habit to train his students to make quick choices. He explained his strategy:

"On the first or second day of school I'd always offer a choice that was likely to create some debate among the group. It often involved working on something individually or as a group or deciding which of two projects the students believed we should start with first.

"They always ended up debating and hemming and hawing. After about five or ten seconds, I say, 'This is so sad. I offer choices like this when people can choose quickly.' Then I'd make the choice for them. Staying consistent with this guideline made the rest of the year go much more smoothly."

AVOID GIVING "CHOICES" THAT ARE ACTUALLY THREATS

People who think they understand Love and Logic... but really don't... often fall into the habit of providing choices such as these:

- "Settle down or go to the principal's office."
- "You can either stop doing that or lose points."
- "You can make a choice to get to work or get a zero."

Those better versed in the Love and Logic approach understand that threats disguised as choices are still threats.

A Success Story

Chuck had never liked school, generally approaching his scholastic responsibilities with the enthusiasm of a toddler served a plate of stewed spinach. Nevertheless, there wasn't a mean bone in his body.

He just preferred drawing, painting, playing his guitar, and anything else requiring an artistic bent.

Yep. Chuck appeared to be an easygoing dude, rarely getting riled about anything. While his room, his hair, his desk at school, and his academic transcript looked like a town after a tornado, he remained unconcerned.

Chuck's mother was wound tighter than a Timex watch. That was her basic personality. Since she was an accomplished educator with two graduate degrees, it drove her absolutely bonkers that he wasn't more organized and motivated to achieve. As such, she spent massive amounts of time and energy attempting to help him adopt a more orderly and concerned attitude. Unlike her son, she ran hot.

The more Chuck appeared to chill, the more heat his mother radiated, attempting to micromanage his life. Her idea of giving choices was, "Do it now or suffer the consequences." Much to her vexation, he accepted these consequences with his "no worries" attitude.

The Four Steps to Responsibility

1. Give a student the chance to act responsibly. Let a student decide, for example, whether or not to bring his homework assignment in on time.

2. Hope and pray the student makes a mistake. This provides opportunities for the student to have a "real world" learning experience. If the student does not bring the homework assignment in on time, you can empathize, "I'm sorry you didn't get it here on time." But you don't offer any other alternatives. Allow the student to suffer the consequences.

3. Stand back and allow consequences, accompanied by liberal doses of empathy, to do the teaching. Students need to learn that their mistakes hurt them. Empathy or sorrow reduces the chance that the student will spend time thinking about anything but his/her own life and decisions instead of focusing on anger or other emotional reactions of the adult.

4. Give the same task again. This sends the unstated message that you believe he or she is wise enough to learn from the mistake that was made.

As middle school arrived, Mom had no inkling of the turmoil bubbling just beneath her son's laidback exterior. Doubling down on his school issues, she created a well-organized system by which she could monitor what he was assigned in each class. This also allowed her to watch that he completed these assignments and turned them in on time. All seemed right with the world. For a solid month going on two, she policed his work and ensured that it returned to school with him in his backpack. She even bought him nice folders and affixed labels corresponding to each of his class subjects.

Her phone rang. It was Ms. Rosemond, Chuck's English teacher. "Can you come down here for a meeting this week? I'm concerned that Chuck might not pass my class."

Three people sat around an uncomfortably small table: Mom, Ms. Rosemond, and Chuck.

"What's going on here?" Mom demanded in an accusatory tone. "I've made sure he completed all of his papers, and I know he's been bringing them back to school. I check every morning to see if they are in their folders!"

At a loss for words, Ms. Rosemond replied, "I'm so sorry. I'm… not sure." Turning to Chuck she inquired, "Chuck? I haven't seen any of those papers. Do you have any thoughts as to how all of this can be?"

A long silence ensued. Then, facing his mother, Chuck answered, "Mom, you can make me do those papers, but you can't make me hand them in."

Apparently, Chuck was not as easygoing as he appeared. Stuffed deep in his locker were weeks' worth of completed assignments. Stuffed deep in his heart had been years of frustration over feeling bossed around.

Chuck's loving mother immersed herself in the Love and Logic approach. As she did, she learned about the science of control and how she could begin to repair her relationship with her son by providing massive doses of small choices within limits. She also learned that by trying to control her son's life, she wasn't allowing him to make the mistakes required to realize that choices matter… that the quality of his life would be directly impacted by the quality of his choices.

As the two of these wonderful people learned about choices, they also developed an appreciation for the fact that neither could really control the other. What a relief it was for Mom to accept the fact that her super fantastic son thrived on a bit of chaos. It was also refreshing for him to see that his mother was not the enemy… she was just someone who felt out of control if things didn't line up.

Years have passed, and Chuck is now a successful business owner. We're guessing he's probably learned the hard way that a bit of organization and concern is a good thing. What's the best part? He and his mother have a great relationship… one made possible by her realization that everyone… down deep… has a strong need for control.

CHAPTER SIX

Responding to Extremely Disruptive Students

Mr. Kenneth

Mr. Kenneth embraced his school's new positive climate initiative with great enthusiasm. Knowing he was going to have a challenging class, he'd made a list of all of the positive, preventative interventions he could use. He was excited about the possibilities.

On a sheet of paper he wrote:

- Greet them at the door every day.
- Teach routines and procedures so they know what to expect.
- Get students with unique learning needs some additional help.
- Match instructional level with the needs of the student.
- Create a classroom community by ensuring that students engage in cooperative learning and collaborative problem solving.
- Apply "How I Run my Love and Logic Classroom."
- Share some control. Provide plenty of small choices over issues that don't matter much to me.
- Seating chart… identify which students need to be placed where.
- Manage student behavior mostly with small interventions

such as moving toward them, whispering questions, etc. Do this to maintain the flow of instruction so there isn't much downtime while I'm teaching.

- Model empathy and respect so they will see… first hand… the expectations for how they treat each other.
- It all comes down to relationships!

Mr. Kenneth's list of positive, preventative strategies was long, but he figured most of it was simple stuff that paid off big time by saving tons of time and energy dealing with chronic behavior problems.

Connor

Connor arrived at school with his own long list of interventions, indelibly etched on his subconscious mind:

- Don't let 'em get too close.
- Don't let 'em love you.
- Don't even let 'em try to like you.
- Stir things up between other kids.
- Never keep your hands to yourself.
- Keep adults off balance.
- They can't hurt you if they're busy putting out fires all around.
- Remain in control at all costs.
- Don't let your guard down.
- Sit at the desk that squeaks and constantly make negative comments.
- Refuse to do your work.
- Keep them fighting battles they can't win.
- Don't let 'em win.

There are many reasons why some students seem bent on creating chaos in our classrooms. Some, like Connor, have been hurt. Trying to protect themselves, they compulsively attempt to control every situation by acting out. Others have real neurological or developmental disabilities that contribute to severe anxiety, impulsivity, hyperactivity, anger, or learning problems. Still others come from homes or neighborhoods where basic social, emotional, or behavioral skills are not taught or reinforced.

Is it important to remember that there is great hope for all of these students?

Connor and Mr. Kenneth Meet

Instinctively, Connor avoided Mr. Kenneth's attempt to connect with him at the door. Eyes darting to and fro, he appraised the environment and located a seat providing strategic advantage and some loose hardware for maximum squeaking and creaking. From this location, he could diagnose the dynamics of the group, begin to orchestrate minor conflict among his peers, and determine which behaviors would most effectively bring his teacher to his knees. For Connor, the first week to ten days was a learning process. During such time, it was simply part of the plan to let adults have their wonderful honeymoon period.

Mr. Kenneth was a tough nut to crack, mostly because he seemed so bent on remaining positive. Determined to meet the challenge, Connor began a pervasive campaign of chaos beginning with multiple meanderings to the pencil sharpener. There were few strategies more effective than wandering like a lost puppy with broken pencil in hand. There were shins to be kicked, books to be knocked, and trash to be talked. One could always respond to any form of correction with an innocent sounding, "How am I supposed to get to work if my pencil is broke?"

> **LOVE AND LOGIC EXPERIMENT:**
> ### This Is Boring!
>
> STUDENT: "This is boring!"
>
> TEACHER (smiling): "If you think this is boring now, just wait until 2 p.m."

By the second week of school, Connor was beginning to hit his stride. He'd pulled a number of followers into his fold, and was successfully creating a situation where Mr. Kenneth was spending more time dealing with problems than delivering instruction.

Have you ever left school at the end of the day feeling incredibly discouraged? Have you ever found yourself moaning, "I just spent the entire day… and all of my energy… trying to get just one or two kids to behave? And the students who were ready to learn got nothing from me!"

Is it true that educators are seeing ever-increasing numbers of students with overwhelmingly deep social and emotional needs? Is it also true that we can conscientiously apply a wide range of positive and preventative strategies and still find ourselves unable to teach due to such students' disruptive behavior?

Educators are seeing ever-increasing numbers of students with overwhelmingly deep social and emotional needs.

By the third week of school, Mr. Kenneth was having difficulty staying positive about his positive plan. Nevertheless, he was committed to remaining a class act. Teaching his way over to Connor, he briefly paused and whispered in the student's ear, "Connor, will you save that behavior for Mrs. Will's class next period? She really likes that stuff."

Knowing tough kids, Mr. Kenneth knew that a little humor could go a long way. Unfortunately, Connor was tougher than the average grizzly bear. "That is so stupid!" he yelled. "That's not even funny!"

The room became so quiet it was deafening.

Completely lost for a response, Mr. Kenneth replied, "Well… thanks for letting me know," and moved away from Connor and said, "Okay, class… on page nineteen, what did we just learn?"

Are there times when our only positive option in the moment doesn't feel like a very good one?

What Are Our Options?

What's a teacher do when nothing seems to be working and a student (or students) remains so disruptive that he or she cannot teach and the other students cannot learn?

Feeling a bit like a failure, Mr. Kenneth confided in the principal, Dr. Lopez: "I don't know what I'm doing wrong. I've worked hard on building a relationship with him... and all of the things that usually work with difficult students. I even made this list of positive techniques so I'd remain committed to doing them. I mean... it's just that nothing seems to be working, and I can't even teach the other students."

Dr. Lopez replied, "So you're doing everything on this list, and it still isn't working?"

"Yes," Mr. Kenneth nodded. "I've even added a few more that aren't written on there. Like I said, these things usually work really well, but not with this student. It's like he's immune to them."

"That is discouraging," Dr. Lopez agreed. "I know how hard you work for these kids, and I know you really care. I guess one option is to just try harder to reach him and not try so hard to teach the kids who are ready to learn. What are your thoughts on that?"

Eyes wide, Mr. Kenneth replied, "Uh... well... I can't just let the rest of the class suffer... I mean, I'll do anything I can to help Connor, but I can't lose the rest of the class in the process."

Dr. Lopez smiled, and then said, "That's one of the things that makes you such a fine teacher. You care so much about all of the kids and you'll bend over backwards trying to reach the ones who most people simply give up on."

"Thanks, I appreciate that," Mr. Kenneth chuckled.

"What I'm getting at," Dr. Lopez continued, "is that we have to continue to do what we can to help Connor while setting it up so that his behavior can't interfere with the rights of his classmates to feel safe and to learn."

A Tough... But Very Important... Decision to Make

In challenging situations such as these, our options are limited, but the ones we choose to pursue will dramatically affect the welfare of everyone involved... including ourselves. We can choose to:

A. do nothing and allow the disruptive student to hold our classroom hostage.

B. spend all of our time and energy trying to cure the disruptive student while ignoring the needs and rights of the rest of the class.

C. work so hard trying to teach and to provide therapy for the disruptive student that we become burnt out and cynical.

D. continue to help the disruptive student while also setting a healthy limit: "I allow students to remain with the group as long as they can do so without creating a problem."

Short-Term Recovery: Maintaining the Learning Environment

Love and Logic teachers protect the flock. They maintain a calm and productive learning environment by ensuring that no student is allowed to interfere with the learning of others by remaining chronically disruptive. They understand that allowing a student to dominate the classroom is not good for that student... and definitely isn't good for anyone else. Therefore, they understand the following:

Sometimes a disruptive student simply needs to be someplace else... temporarily.

Why?

So the rest of the class has an opportunity to learn and the disrupting student has an opportunity to become calm.

Dr. Lopez handed Mr. Kenneth a booklet she'd received at a recent Love and Logic conference. "I just learned something that might help with this situation. Dr. Fay, at Love and Logic, calls it short-term recovery. He makes the point that sometimes the only option is to have the student go somewhere else. That is, so that we can teach and the other students can learn."

The Only Goal of Short-Term Recovery
Preserve the learning environment so that you can teach and the other students can learn.

"In-school suspension?" Mr. Kenneth asked.

"Oh, no," said Dr. Lopez, "it's not about punishing the student or even trying to help them. It's just about maintaining a healthy learning environment so the rest of the class can learn." Pointing at page eight in the booklet she continued, "Check this out. This gives an overview."

Mr. Kenneth scanned the page.

Preserving the Classroom Learning Environment

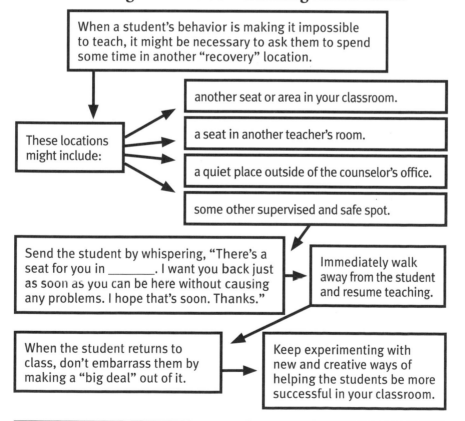

When a student's behavior is making it impossible to teach, it might be necessary to ask them to spend some time in another "recovery" location.

These locations might include:

- another seat or area in your classroom.
- a seat in another teacher's room.
- a quiet place outside of the counselor's office.
- some other supervised and safe spot.

Send the student by whispering, "There's a seat for you in _____. I want you back just as soon as you can be here without causing any problems. I hope that's soon. Thanks."

Immediately walk away from the student and resume teaching.

When the student returns to class, don't embarrass them by making a "big deal" out of it.

Keep experimenting with new and creative ways of helping the students be more successful in your classroom.

"Wow, that's quite a flow chart," Mr. Kenneth replied.

"Yes," Dr. Lopez laughed. "Dr. Fay admitted that. But I do think it gives us some baseline ideas for how we might deal with the current situation. What do you think?"

Taking another look at the page, Mr. Kenneth answered, "I think the basic idea makes sense, but there seems to be a lot of potential loose ends. Like… what if he refuses to leave? Or… what if he likes to go and just acts out to leave class?"

Dr. Lopez answered, "That's right. At the conference, Dr. Fay gave us a number of potential answers to those loose ends. He also encouraged us to consider all the details before putting this plan into action. He calls it 'plugging the holes before you launch the boat.' This current situation with Connor seems like a great opportunity to experiment with this. If you're interested, we can do some brainstorming."

Mr. Kenneth nodded, "Oh yes! The wonderful thing about Connor is that he's made me highly motivated to learn something new."

Making a Plan

Success in implementing short-term recovery involves first asking a variety of questions pertaining to how it applies in your unique classroom and school. When the questions are asked, potential solutions will follow.

When Should They Be Sent?

In the vast majority of cases, short-term recovery should not be the first resort. A student is asked to go only after it's clear that other preventative techniques are not working. With this said, it's also essential that common sense be applied. Does it make sense for a teacher to spend significant portions of time attempting every preventative measure under the sun while failing to spend much of any time teaching? Does it make any practical sense for a student to believe they can't be asked to leave unless their teacher has completed a long list of positive interventions? Clearly the answer to these questions is "no."

Educators who understand the Love and Logic approach strive to strike a healthy balance between meeting the needs of each student and the needs of the overall group. Therefore, they do their best to help misbehaving students remain in class while at the same time remembering that their primary responsibility is to teach the entire group. They strive to live each day knowing they've done their best to help troubled students while protecting the rights of those who arrived in class that day ready to learn.

Short-Term Recovery is not intended to...

- be used as a first resort.
- be done in a humiliating or punitive fashion.
- be used as a consequence designed to set students straight.
- cure students' emotional or behavioral problems.
- make students do their papers or other academic work.

Should They be Sent for Refusing to Complete their Work?

No. We'll repeat it. If a student is not completing their work *but* isn't making it difficult for others to do so, they should remain with the class. Short-term recovery was never intended to be used as a strategy for motivating underachieving or apathetic students. In chapter nine, we'll address this complex issue.

If a student is not completing their work and is creating problems for others, that's a different story. The student may need to spend some time in recovery because of their disruptive behavior... not because of their lack of motivation or failure to complete assignments.

How Should Students Be Sent?

As we learned in chapter one, correcting students from across the room is one of the surest ways to end up fighting endless power struggles. When we violate a student's dignity by embarrassing them in front of their peers, we shouldn't be surprised when they counter with a less-than-respectful behavior. Wise teachers gradually teach their way toward misbehaving students, taking great care to approach with a whisper and a question: "Are you going to be able to settle down, or will you need to leave for a while? You decide."

The split second "you decide" leaves their mouth, these teachers move away from the misbehaving student and resume teaching. An unstated, yet powerfully clear message is the result:

"I care so deeply about you that I don't want to cause you any embarrassment or humiliation. I also care about you enough to set some limits. And… by the way… I can handle these sorts of things without breaking a sweat."

When the situation is handled with this type of finesse, students often choose to remain with the group by improving their behavior. This is always the desired result. However, when they don't, it's up to the teacher to once again teach and move… teach and move… their way back within whisper range, to say: "Oh… Mrs. Tomlinson has a seat for you across the hall. That's room 202. Come back as soon as you can be here without causing a problem. I hope that's soon. Thanks."

Observers of Love and Logic teachers quickly see a pattern. They see these teachers teaching while moving… teaching while moving… teaching while moving. They see them teaching and moving even up to the split second they briefly stop and whisper something to a student. As soon as the whispering is over, they immediately move away from the student and resume teaching… as if nothing ever happened.

Where Can They Go?

The Love and Logic approach was inspired by the real needs and practical limitations faced by classroom educators. Some schools have well-developed short-term recovery plans where specific locations are set aside for students who need some "time away" from the group. In many other schools, however, teachers find themselves having to be a lot more creative and resourceful.

Over the years, educators have shared a wide variety of highly creative options:

> *"I found that with my first graders, a beach umbrella works really great. I have it set up in the back of the classroom. We even painted a beach scene on the wall. Oftentimes I can simply ask a student to 'spend some time at the beach.'"*

> *"Our school had no plan for recovery, but three of us in our hall started helping each other… pretty much informally. If I had a student who needed some recovery time, I could send them next-door or across the hall to an empty seat in one of those teachers' classrooms. If they needed to send a student my way, that was fine, too."*

> *"Our school counselor and our assistant principal helped us out. They made some spots available where students could sit and just cool their heels. The adults would just go on with their paperwork or phone calls as the students just sat there."*

> *"Within our preschool, sometimes a little one would do recovery by having to follow the director around the school as she made her rounds. The director made it really dull for them as they walked from spot to spot. As soon as they seemed a bit calmer, she'd drop the child back at their classroom."*

The key requirements for an effective short-term recovery spot are few but important. First, and most obviously, the location should be supervised. This doesn't mean the student receives intensive one-on-one attention. It simply means there is an adult nearby who's aware of where the student is and what they are doing. We don't recommend using the hall as a recovery spot. I (Charles) learned this the hard way. I discovered, much to my chagrin, that one of our students always managed to need some hall time at the exact same moment his buddies did from nearby classrooms. Why? We discovered them playing catch in the hall. The three of them even brought their baseball gloves to school!

Secondly, and also rather obvious, is that the location should not be exciting for the student. On occasion, some students find too many friends in the classroom where they've been sent. One teacher commented, "We had to stop sending one of ours across the hall because her sister was in that class along with many of her followers. Allowing her to have recovery in a room with a class one grade level above solved this problem."

The main office, where the hustle and bustle of daily activity is taking place, is not typically a choice location for recovery. We've seen many students turn this location into either a battlefield or an opportunity to build exciting new relationships. If the main office in your school is rather dull and uneventful... and you are blessed with a wonderful Love and Logic style secretary... you might give it a shot. If not, find another spot.

What Should They Do There?

Short-term recovery is not designed to be a punishment or a consequence. It's not intended to be an opportunity for students to receive counseling or to solve problems. It's not meant to motivate students into completing their schoolwork.

Short-term recovery has only two goals:

#1. Maintain a calm learning environment so the rest of the class can learn.

#2. Provide the disruptive student with an opportunity to get calmed down.

Too frequently, well-meaning educators shoot themselves in the foot. They do so by turning recovery into a counseling, problem-solving, or disciplinary session. When this happens, the disruptive student is now receiving even more adult attention as a result of misbehaving. Have you noticed how rewarding this becomes for many challenging kids? Have you also noticed how many of these challenging students relish the thought of sparring with adults under such circumstances? Have you also discovered how poorly discussions proceed when one or more of the people involved are experiencing emotional fight or flight?

Are there many students who'd rather engage in one-on-one discussion than do their work? Do these kids learn to get incredibly skilled at avoidance when they know this option is available? One student put it well: "Talking about your problems sure beats doing math."

When they go to recovery, students are given the time and space to recover. Adults provide minimum attention and save discussions for calmer times. To be clear, this doesn't mean that students don't receive counseling or other forms of effective help. What it means is that wise adults provide this attention and assistance at a later time.

> One teacher commented, "We made the mistake of expecting all students to complete a problem-solving form before they could return to class from recovery. It wasn't long before we were discovering that this created more problems than it solved. Students were missing a lot more class than necessary, and we were spending crazy amounts of time trying to keep track of forms and trying to make the kids complete them. Things got way better when we decided to make recovery and problem solving separate experiences."

How Long Should They Stay?

Short-term recovery is not in-school suspension or detention. Most of the time, students remain just long enough to get themselves back together mentally, emotionally, or behaviorally. That's why we call it short-term recovery. Highly effective Love and Logic teachers make this clear as they are asking the student to leave:

"I want you back here as soon as possible. Come back as soon as you can be here without causing a problem. I hope that's soon."

Of course there are times when a student may return when they are not truly ready to be there without causing a problem. When this occurs, there are a few options, depending upon the specifics of the situation. The teacher may ask the student to return to recovery and come back when they are completely sure they are ready. The student may be assigned to recovery for the remainder of the class period or even the school day. In rare cases, the student may even be required to complete a plan before they are allowed to return to class. This last option, as we discussed above, should not be used with every instance of recovery and should not involve the student receiving significant amounts of involvement from adults. It should simply require some thinking and work on the part of the student with perhaps a few brief suggestions provided by a rather disinterested adult bystander:

"It's a bummer that you can't go back to class without giving your teacher a plan. Well… I guess one idea is to sit someplace where there's not so much temptation to talk."

Again, when a student is in recovery, even when it has to be extended, there is great care and wisdom given toward using few words and expecting the student to own and solve the problem. In-depth problem solving, counseling, or therapeutic intervention can take place at another time... when it doesn't allow kids to actively avoid participation in class.

But... What If They Won't Go?

Mr. Kenneth and Dr. Lopez spent nearly an hour after school, beginning to develop a short-term recovery plan they could use with Connor. Mr. Kenneth was beginning to have some ideas about how it might look, but he still had one major question: "What do I do if he says something like, 'You can't make me leave,' or if he just crosses his arms and refuses to go?"

Consequences for Going to Short-Term Recovery?

Teachers often ask, "Should I provide an additional consequence when a student requires a trip to short-term recovery?

No.

Educators have enough to worry about without having to come up with additional consequences.

Most of the time better progress is achieved when we ask the student, "What do you think you could do to help yourself need fewer trips to recovery? I'd really like to help. We miss you when you aren't here."

Chapter eight provides a process for guiding students toward owning and solving problems such as these.

Dr. Lopez smiled. "Based on what you've told me about this student, it seems like the chances are high that something like that will happen. At the conference, Dr. Fay suggested we ought to hope and pray that a student gets really nasty and refuses to leave."

Now Mr. Kenneth was confused. "What? For what conceivable reason would we want to do that?"

Dr. Lopez continued, "Dr. Fay gave us a plan for handling this situation without breaking a sweat. When a teacher can do this, it really gains them respect and admiration from their students. I need to leave in about ten minutes. Would you like to hear what he suggested?"

Mr. Kenneth's astonished expression turned to a grin as he replied, "I can do that!"

"It's Time"

The next morning, Mr. Kenneth awoke before his alarm. Driving to school, he rehearsed his plan. "Step one," he thought, "is to let the teachers in my hallway know what might happen. Then I'll tell Dr. Lopez that the plan is a go. Then I'll visit with the three students. Let's see… Hunter… Chloe… and… Jasmine. Yeah, those three will do fine."

Like every other day of the year, Mr. Kenneth stood at the doorway of his classroom, greeting each and every student as they entered. Connor slid by in his typical way doing everything he could to avoid connecting. Plunking down at his desk, he immediately turned to his neighbor, and said, "Man… do you have any mirrors in your house?"

"What do you mean? What's your problem?" the other student replied.

"If you did," Connor answered with a shove, "you'd know how stupid you look."

Laugher filled the area, most of it from students who knew that if they weren't laughing, they'd become the target of Connor's abuse.

Mr. Kenneth whispered into Connor's ear, "I allow students to remain with the group as long as they can do so without causing any problems. Thanks." Remembering his discussion with Dr. Lopez, he immediately moved away and started the day: "Okay, guys, it's great to see you! I bet you couldn't wait to get back here and learn some more algebra."

Connor wasn't thrilled by algebra, and he definitely was not impressed with Mr. Kenneth's "I allow students to remain with the group…" comment. Now he was sliding one of the legs of his desk ever so deliberately back and forth across the floor. Screech… scratch… screech… scratch… screech… scratch. The grin on Connor's face as he performed this water torture temporarily left Mr. Kenneth fantasizing about illegal behavior management strategies.

Mr. Kenneth quickly adjusted his own attitude and began the lesson: "So… can anybody tell me what snowboarding and algebraic equations have in common?"

Moving gradually in Connor's direction, he scanned the room for hands. "Yes… Trystan."

Trystan answered, "They have to have good balance."

"You got it!" Mr. Kenneth replied. "Equations need to be balanced. Both sides of the equation need to be equal."

Another hand shot up. Mr. Kenneth responded, "Yes, Hector."

"Is that why they call them equations? Is it because the sides have to equate?"

Mr. Kenneth was nearing his destination: Connor's desk. "Yes, Hector. That's a really good observation."

With empathy, Mr. Kenneth leaned toward Connor's ear, and whispered, "Oh, man… this is unfortunate. Mr. King has a seat for you next-door. It's room 109. Come back as soon as you can be here without causing a problem. I hope that's soon. Thanks."

You guessed it. As soon as the word "Thanks" rolled off his tongue, Mr. Kenneth moved away and resumed the lesson: "So we see the problem on page nine, Y divided by nineteen equals one hundred seventy-three. What's the first step in…?"

"I'm not going! You can't tell me what to do!" Connor was emphatic.

Mr. Kenneth provided an academy award-winning performance. Acting cool as a cucumber, he moved toward his three helpers: Hunter, Chloe, and Jasmine. "It's time," he said. "You know what to do."

"It's time" meant that Hunter was to head quickly next-door and then to the office, with the purpose of letting that teacher and the administrative staff know that Mr. Kenneth had a "situation."

"It's time" meant that Chloe and Jasmine would be in charge of leading the entire class to the emergency safe spot outside. Per his plan with Dr. Lopez, an adult would meet them in the hall to supervise the exodus.

"Okay, class… line up." Mr. Kenneth continued, "Just follow Chloe and Jasmine."

They Don't Have to be an Actor When There's no Audience

Sometimes the only option is to have a student removed while his or her peers are still present. Nevertheless, the process typically unfolds in a much calmer and safer manner when there's no audience to witness the event. Can you imagine being backed into a corner in front of your peers? Can you imagine feeling that the only way you can preserve your reputation is to come out scratching and clawing?

At the Love and Logic conference she attended, Dr. Lopez learned the importance of removing the audience in these extreme situations. She also learned that the students are far more likely to leave peacefully with someone other than the teacher they are working their hardest to defy. The teacher's role in this situation is to supervise the student until someone else arrives to remove them. Their role is not to reason with the student or to even say a word. Their role is also to stay out of the way if the student refuses to remain in the room.

LOVE AND LOGIC EXPERIMENT:
Proactive Recovery

TEACHER: "I've noticed that you seem to have a hard time getting calmed down right after changing activities and returning to my class. Do you think this is a challenging time for you?"

STUDENT: "Uh… I guess. Everybody's crowding and bumping into me in the hall."

TEACHER: "If you feel that you need some time to calm down before coming in, feel free to go to Ms. Jacob's room before coming here. You won't be in trouble… just join us as soon as you can. I miss you when you're not here."

NOTE: Ironically, teachers who've used this with a student almost universally remark that the student doesn't choose to put themselves in recovery… yet is calmer and better behaved.

Connor temporarily slid down in his chair. Watching the class leave, a lightbulb formed over his head. "Hey," he yelled, "I'm going with them!"

Mr. Kenneth was prepared. Catching up with the class, he proclaimed, "Change of plan. Let's all head to the office."

Like many pizza restaurants, florists, and the U.S. Postal System, effective teachers are more than willing to deliver. By the time Connor realized what had happened, he was just seconds from Dr. Lopez's office. Stepping into the hall, she whispered to Connor, "It seems like you're really having a hard day. I have a spot where nobody will bother you."

When Students Feed Off Each Other

Teachers often find themselves in the frustrating situation in which more than one student is misbehaving. The teacher in this situation finds him/herself unable to deal effectively with one child because others are interrupting or supporting the misbehaving youngster.

Experiment with the following process for solving the problem:

Make a list of the students involved and prioritize the list. Put the most compliant of the students at the top of the list and the least compliant at the bottom.

Divide and conquer. Arrange with fellow teachers to provide a seat in the rear of their classrooms so you can send the students, one at a time, to these separate areas. You will need one room for each student. These students will not be expected to participate with the other class. Each goes with the understanding that he/she may return to class when that will not result in any form of disruption.

Meet with the principal to describe your solution and ask for support. "I am doing this because I cannot allow these children to disrupt the class. I don't want to make a problem for you, so if any one of these children acts out in the temporary classroom, I'd like him/her to come to you for a 'cool-down' period. Please don't feel a need to do anything other than allow the student to cool down and then return to my class when ready."

When the disruption starts, you have two options. If you are able to move the group leader to another location, do so first. Then say to the other students involved, "Do you guys think you can get yourselves back together, or do I need to find another place for you?"

If you question the ease with which you can remove the leader, approach the most compliant student on your list and say, "That is not acceptable. Mr. Sawyer has a place in his room for you until you can get yourself back together. You may return when you know you can be here without causing a problem. Thank you."

As soon as this student leaves the room, go to the next most compliant student on the list and say, "Mrs. Babcock is expecting you in her room. You may return as soon as you can be here without causing a problem. Thank you."

Continue this process until you get to the last student (least compliant) and say, "Now, do you think you can behave here, or would you rather go to a different room until you can? Thank you."

Of course, it's often helpful to send another student to make sure the individuals have gone to their assigned rooms.

Implement the One-Sentence Intervention. Review the steps for this intervention beginning on page 64. Start noticing positive and personal attributes, placing most of your emphasis on the students playing the largest role in the problem. Mention them in private. For example, "Jeremy, I noticed you are really interested in baseball cards." Do this a couple of times per week for three weeks.

Experiment with the following when this student starts to misbehave: "Jeremy, will you stop doing that, just for me? Thank you." Students who've bonded with their teacher are far more cooperative.

Start having "heart to heart" talks with these students after school. Meet with them one at a time. The idea here is not to solve the problem all at once, but to plant some seeds in the student's mind:

TEACHER: "Jeremy, I noticed that you've been having a hard time behaving when you're around your friends. Are you aware that this makes it difficult for me to teach?"

JEREMY: "I guess."

TEACHER: "There are several reasons why this happens with some kids. Sometimes it's because they hate the teacher, sometimes they're afraid the work is too hard, sometimes it's because the kids are part of organized crime, sometimes it's because things aren't going well at home, and sometimes it's because the kids need friends so badly that they're willing to act out in class to be part of the group. Does anything sound familiar to you?"

JEREMY: "I don't know."

TEACHER: "Thanks for giving it some thought. I'll see you."

Continue the "heart to heart" talks until a better relationship is developed.

If the student continues to act out, the following conversation may be helpful:

TEACHER: "Say, Jeremy, I didn't see a great improvement in your behavior today. Do you hate me?"

JEREMY: "No."

TEACHER: "Guess what it looks like to me."

JEREMY: "I don't know."

TEACHER: "I'm thinking that either I have done something terrible that you don't want to tell me about, or you need your friends so badly, you have to continue to act up just to look good to them. I'm wondering if you'd be happier sitting in a different spot. What are your thoughts?"

These steps often solve the problem. If they don't, consider reassigning one or more of these students. There are times when the best solution is to break up the group. It never serves the best interests of the child, the class, or the teacher for a group to stay together when it has become dysfunctional. This is a time when the teacher needs to set aside personal feelings of "not wanting to give up" on the child or problem.

Although this solution involves the use of recovery and other skills, it's always essential to remember that the single most powerful factor remains the quality of the relationship between the teacher and the student.

Recovery: A Bandage not a Cure

Occasionally, we'll hear, "Short-term recovery isn't working."

After inquiring, "Tell us more," we usually hear some variation on one or both of the following:

"The student keeps acting out. He isn't learning anything from recovery."

"She likes going to recovery. She seems to get sent there on purpose so she can avoid doing her work."

As noted above, short-term recovery was never developed to do anything other than allow educators to maintain a calm learning environment when one or more disruptive students are not responding to preventative interventions. While there are certainly times when students do learn important lessons from experiencing recovery, it was never developed for this purpose.

Short-term recovery is a bandage… not a cure.

What does common sense dictate when we've cut one of our fingers and it begins to bleed? Most of us would agree, "Put a bandage on it."

Let's consider one possible outcome of this first aid: The finger begins to heal and all is well with the world. Was the healing mostly attributable to the bandage, or was it most likely due to the fact that the cut was minor and there was no underlying infection?

> **LOVE AND LOGIC EXPERIMENT:**
> ### The Secret Signal
>
> If a student needs frequent trips to recovery, experiment with creating a secret signal that only you and the student recognize.
>
> This signal avoids embarrassing the student while prompting them to either calm down at their seat or go to a recovery setting.

Sometimes even the most skilled educators need a quick solution for protecting their class from chronic disruptions. Since some of the students they use recovery with aren't troubled by deep wounds or underlying social, emotional, or neurological illness, they begin to need time away from the class less and less. Is this because the bandage (i.e. recovery) cured them, or is it because these students aren't deeply wounded or ill in the first place?

Let's consider a second possible outcome of bandaging our wounded finger: After a few days, it begins to swell, throbs like crazy, and oozes puss. Yuck! Was this state of affairs caused by the bandage, or was it the result of a deeper wound with serious infection? Should we see a doctor?

Sometimes students continue to act out, or even get worse, after a highly loving, effective teacher uses short-term recovery. Does this mean the bandage (i.e. recovery) caused the problem, or is it because of deep wounds or serious illness? Does this child need more help than even the most skilled teacher can provide?

The effectiveness of short-term recovery is determined by one brief question: "Does it allow me to continue teaching the students who are ready to learn?" If this is the case, recovery is working.

Obviously, great educators never give up on kids. While they may need to use short-term recovery with a student quite frequently, they also collaborate with their team, other professionals, and the child's parents to identify hypotheses regarding why the student is hurting so badly that they cannot be successful in the classroom.

You aren't the doctor, but you can be a wonderful part of the treatment team. Always remember there is hope for these students. Always remind yourself that they need to have a relationship with you as a calm and loving authority figure. This is only possible when they see you're strong enough to protect the flock in loving ways. This will only happen when they see that their trips to recovery don't change the fact that they are truly loved and valued. This means when the student returns from recovery, we smile instead of frown, and don't attempt to complicate matters by setting them straight with extra consequences.

CHAPTER SEVEN

Managing Your Class...
Instead of
It Managing You

Mark's Special Teacher

Mark was like Bigfoot. Few had actually gotten a good look at him but many believed. The reason he was so rarely spotted was the rapidity with which he moved about the school and classroom... somewhat like an F-4 tornado spinning and kicking up dust in its path. Suggesting that Mark had the hyperactivity, impulsivity, and inattention of a child with true ADHD was like saying the sinking of the *Titanic* was kind of a downer.

As a school psychologist, I was assigned to observe him as he transitioned to a new classroom dedicated to meeting the needs of such students. Ms. Matsuoka, or "Ms. M." as her students referred to her, was a master at working with the most hyperkinetic, least self-controlled students. Because of her hard work and dedication with such children, she was rewarded by the school district with a classroom full of them.

There I sat with my behavior observation instrument and sharpened number two pencil. The first thing I noticed was not Mark, but how Ms. M. moved about the classroom as she rarely missed a beat with her lesson. As Mark began to vibrate, she moved gracefully his way continuing to teach. Still delivering instruction, her hand rested gently on his shoulder. His vibration stopped. As soon as it did, she moved to another wiggling student, pausing briefly and whispering to him, "Shaun, I'd like to hear how your baseball game went on Saturday. Will you tell me about it after class?" Shaun stopped wiggling.

I'm embarrassed to say that my observation of Mark was quite poor. Ms. M.'s finesse was just too distracting. Moving from Shaun, she ventured… always continuing to teach… toward two students who were beginning to argue. Whispering with a smile, she quickly asked, "Brenda, will you please go tell the janitor about the heat? It feels warm in here. Come back quickly. Ramie, I forgot to return the library books stacked on my desk. Will you take them down and drop them in the return? Thanks." Both students jumped to their tasks, and Ms. M. continued her lesson on adverbs.

Mark and Shaun were once again starting to vibrate. Ms. M., always on the move, headed their way. Leaning over, she quietly said, "Guys, I'm really interested in how many positions you can do your work in today. Feel free to do it standing up, sitting down, one knee on the seat, or any other way that doesn't cause a problem for anyone else." This bought her a few more seconds of calm.

As I watched, I realized that Ms. M. wasn't making much of a big deal out of anything… other than constantly buying herself a few more moments of teaching time.

Now she was on to Marcelle, who was sniffing his desk instead of working. I bet you guessed it! She did so as she continued to instruct. With a gentle pat on the back, she whispered, "Oh, Marcelle, I just love having you in my class. Is there something I can help you with? Come with me as we talk." There was Marcelle, following Ms. M. as she continued about the room, teaching and buying herself more time to do it.

"Ms. M., I don't like this writing stuff. It's too hard," he complained.

She empathized while moving back toward his desk. "It can be really challenging. When I have a chance, you can walk with me again, and I'll give you some ideas about how to get it done."

As she moved away, Marcelle's face told the entire story: He had that happy and somewhat dazed look that only happens when a student likes their teacher too much to create a stink. Yes, Ms. M. was a master.

> **LOVE AND LOGIC EXPERIMENT:**
> ## I Can't Do It!
>
> STUDENT: "I can't do it! It's too hard."
>
> TEACHER: "Aren't you glad I don't believe that?"

What Do Love and Logic Teachers Look Like?

If you're looking for big-time excitement and riveting drama, don't watch a Love and Logic teacher. It's simply not that exciting... unless of course, you love seeing teachers who know the art and science of maintaining order without spending much time on heavy-duty discipline.

Many skilled Love and Logic teachers have been accused... by their less-skilled peers... of being handed a classroom full of "easy" students. Why? Because it often looks to the unsophisticated eye like they aren't doing much. It's like the kids are just behaving. Upon closer inspection, the wiser observer sees that such educators have stacked the deck in favor of success by consistently performing a number of rather small, yet powerfully preventative interventions.

Successful classroom managers focus on prevention.

Less successful ones focus on detention.

Laying the Foundation

If the foundation is weak, the house will fall. Sadly, some teachers and schools are feeling so rushed to dive into the curriculum and get students prepared for success on tests that they are skipping the vital bedrock required for creating calm, high-achieving school and classroom cultures. The word *culture* can be defined as a group's collectively agreed upon way of doing things. When we have a culture, we do things in certain ways because we've come to the conclusion that these ways are the best ways. We also have a culture because we've practiced these ways so frequently they've become automatic.

For example, good drivers have a culture of getting to and fro in their automobiles. Since stopping at red lights and proceeding at green ones leads to a smoother, safer, and more predictable experience for everyone, stepping on the brake for red and on the accelerator for green has become automatic. Again, this "culture" requires that we have some agreed upon ways and have practiced them toward the point of automaticity.

A classroom or school without a culture is like a busy city filled with drivers holding different ideas about red lights versus green ones... stop signs versus yield signs, turn lanes versus through lanes, etc.

Build Positive Relationships

The foundation of all successful work with students involves creating a classroom culture based on positive relationships. This, without any doubt, is the Love and Logic way. We hope that throughout this book you see how all aspects of Love and Logic are designed to build... or at least maintain... positive teacher-student relationships.

The first place to start when struggling with a difficult student or class is to implement the one-sentence intervention discussed in chapter three. Teachers are frequently amazed at how such a simple technique can have such a tremendous impact. A school principal recently commented:

> *"Josh had been kicked out of three or four schools by the time he ended up in our alternative school. Honestly, we were all a bit concerned and were bracing ourselves for the worst. During his first week with us, he practically burned through my entire team of eighth grade teachers. We decided that all of us would begin to reply with massive amounts of empathy and find at least one unique and special thing we could notice about him every day. That was six people noticing special things about him every day! After a week, he went home and told his mom that we were all crazy but it was the only school he'd ever liked. I think this worked because he had probably never before had teachers who noticed anything other than his disruptiveness."*

Avoid Blow-ups and Battles over Learning and Work Completion

Many classroom disruptions begin when conscientious educators attempt to make students do their work. Chapter nine is entirely dedicated to addressing the subject of reaching unmotivated students.

Too frequently, conscientious educators resort to lectures or threats when a student refuses to complete their work. Sadly, this often results in power struggles and disruptions that interfere with the flow of instruction and the maintenance of a calm, productive classroom culture. Educators always enjoy greater success when they briefly whisper to the student, "How can I help?" instead of "You need to get to work" or "If you don't get to work, then_____."

LOVE AND LOGIC EXPERIMENT:
Lost Homework

STUDENT: "I don't have my homework. I lost it."

TEACHER: "That's really sad, but the good news is that I'll be happy to accept it tomorrow for reduced credit."

Whispering "How can I help?" usually does not immediately light a powerful motivational fire within the student. Nevertheless, it does allow us to avoid battles that can end up sabotaging our ability to manage the classroom. In chapter nine, you'll see that helping students get motivated to learn and complete work has nothing to do with nagging, threatening, or providing consequences. It has everything to do with meeting underlying emotional needs that free the brain's inborn drive to learn and achieve.

How We Do Things Here

Early in her career, Ms. M. also discovered that many of her students were coming from homes where they were not learning the basic behavioral skills essential for school success. Some had never learned how to sit quietly in a chair, stand in line, wait, stop, or go. They were a bit like U.S. drivers suddenly plunked in the middle of London… where chaps drive on the other side of the road. Many had never learned how to enter a group without yelling, "What's up?" Quite a few believed it was standard operating procedure, and well within acceptable societal standards to announce their need for a trip to the restroom by yelling, "I really got to take a _____!" Still more believed that settling disputes with fists rather than words was the best way. They weren't bad kids. They were kids who hadn't yet learned the "culture" of school.

We used to emphasize the importance of teaching preschool, kindergarten, and elementary students how to behave at school. We used to suggest that educators of younger students spend most of the first days… even month of school… working on these behavioral and social skills *before* focusing on the academic curriculum. Nowadays things are different. Now we urge educators of *all* grade levels, including middle school, high school, and even college, to never ever assume that their students have the basic kindergarten skills required for success.

We realize this is not a novel concept confined to the Love

and Logic approach. In fact, practically every good classroom management book ever written has included some discussion of teaching behavioral routines and procedures. The great work on this subject by Harry Wong comes to mind. This is old-school stuff. With that admitted, we can't bring ourselves to skip at least a brief discussion of the subject. Why? Simply because it's more relevant than ever *and* educators are feeling more pressure to skip it so they can get further ahead in the academic curricula: Bad idea. In reality, we position our students to be further ahead academically when we spend less time on academics and more time early in the year on behavior.

Over the years, Ms. M. developed a beginning of the year planning strategy designed to help her remember what she called "School Success Skills." Just before school started every year, she completed her worksheet. It reminded her to ask herself three questions:

1. If I had perfectly behaved students, what would it look like as they were doing the following?
   - Entering and beginning class.
   - Ending and leaving class.
   - Transitioning to other activities.
   - Walking in the hall.
   - Solving problems related to forgotten, lost, or "stolen" books, supplies, possessions, etc.
   - Dealing with teasing or bullying.
   - Asking to use the restroom.
   - Sharpening pencils.
   - Etc.

2. How can I teach these behaviors using direct instruction, modeling, and plenty of practice?

3. How can I set and enforce limits that communicate the importance of these behaviors?

Ms. M. was dedicated to creating a culture of calmness in her classroom but was sensitive to the fact that it was not her role to expect her students to abandon how they operated once they left school grounds. "How do we do things *here*?" was the question she consistently asked her students. Other questions she asked: "How do we ask to use the restroom *here*? How do we solve problems with each other *here*? How do we get ready to leave the classroom *here*? What tone and volume of voice do we use *here*? How do we act when we are entering a room *here*?"

The First Minute or Two Will Make it or Break it

Great teachers like Ms. M. know their starting routine for each and every day is like the wonderful signs we see when we enter a new state. "Welcome to Kansas" or "Welcome to Maine" or "You are entering Florida, the Sunshine State." These indicate that we are moving into a different place... where there might be some different ways of doing things.

The State of Kansas trained me very quickly to abide by their different highway "culture."

Interstate 70 through Eastern Colorado is about as stimulating as standing in line at your local motor vehicle department. Fortunately, the speed limit is 75 miles per hour, so one has the ongoing sense that "this too shall pass." Numb from the tedium of the drive, I failed to notice the sign indicating that we'd entered Kansas. I also failed to note the reduction in speed limit from 75 to 70 MPH.

The state trooper was quite friendly as he handed me my ticket. There were no lectures, threats, or anything else that might damage my self-esteem. This made things even worse. At least if he'd been nasty, I could have somehow blamed him for the problem. Bummer. And... the matter wasn't made any easier by the innocent, yet annoying chatter coming out of the backseat from our four-year-old: "What's happening? What is going on?

Mommy? Is Daddy gonna get put in jail? This is so sad, Daddy. Daddy, didn't you see the sign? Daddy… it's okay. You have some money… Daddy… Daddy."

It was amazing how quickly this modified my behavior. I set the cruise control at sixty-nine. A courteous and friendly guy… concerned about my safety… completely changed my behavior by enforcing one simple limit.

If this wonderful state trooper had not enforced the law, would I have believed that Kansas was a different place from Colorado? Have you ever known a teacher who failed to prove to his or her students that their classroom was a different place than the hall, the playground, the neighborhood, etc.? Have you known an educator who consistently allowed their students to enter the room out of control… and therefore trained his or her students that out-of-control behavior was the culture of their room?

When a behavior is repeatedly performed in a certain context, that context serves to cue that behavior.

When students are allowed to enter a classroom acting out of control, the threshold of that classroom begins to cue out-of-control behavior.

Highly effective teachers provide a welcome sign for the classroom each and every day. This sign not only provides a warm greeting but also gives their students a clear indication that they are moving into a different place with a different culture. Let's see how Ms. M. handled this brief, yet supremely important part of the day.

Greeting with the Elements of Human Bonding

A teacher is not a Love and Logic teacher if he or she does not stand outside of their classroom door, greeting students at the beginning of each and every class. Love and Logic educators also know the importance of providing eye contact, smiles, and handshakes/high-fives. When we provide these fundamental elements of human bonding, do we save ourselves a lot of headaches later on? Did Ms. M. understand her students were less likely to create problems if they felt emotionally connected to her?

Humor

Ms. M. also understood that caring humor and fun are essential emotional needs. Because of this she'd often joke with her students as she greeted them:

> *"Oh, it's so good to see you! I was wondering if I should be boring today or not boring. What do you think?"*

> *"It's great to see you. I noticed that your legs go all the way to the ground today."*

> *"We missed you. I was wondering if you could give me a hard time today so that I can work on my skills. What do you think?" (She'd learned that students have a much harder time hassling her when they're asked to do so.)*

A Simple Limit or Two

Ms. M. was famous among students for having a set-in-stone limit about entering her room: "I allow students to come into my classroom as soon as they are calm." She had this limit for two reasons:

- She understood that her students needed to see she was dedicated to providing a calm and orderly experience.
- She knew if she allowed a wildly acting student to cross the threshold, the context of her room would signal wild behavior.

Observing her greeting routine, I (Charles) was fortunate to see her enforce this limit with Mark. Coming down the hall like a puppy on pep pills, he encountered her at the door. "Hello, Mark!" she greeted him with friendly enthusiasm and a bit of volume. Quickly shifting gears, she leaned toward his ear and quietly asked, "Oh… Mark… when do I allow students to enter my room?"

Mark smiled. "When we are calm?" he questioned, quickly transforming from a wiggling wonder to a comparatively calm young man.

Producing a high-five, Ms. M. replied in an enthusiastic whisper, "You got it… and it looks like you're ready. Come on in."

Ms. M., like that wonderful Kansas State Trooper, demonstrated two things as students entered her "state." The first being, "I'm glad you're here." The second being, "I care about your safety."

Productivity

Ms. M. also believed that the threshold of her classroom… like the signs we often see on streets and highways… should indicate "Work Zone Ahead."

As students entered, they always encountered a brief review assignment that could only be completed during the first five minutes of class. Too many teachers wait for everyone to get into the room before work begins. Wiser ones understand that downtime at the beginning of class is the kiss of death.

Ms. M.'s beginning of class assignment was always rather simple and easy for all students to complete. It was also worth real points toward her students' grades and couldn't be made up if missed due to lateness or failure to stay on task.

Predictability

We once met a teacher who indicated that most of what she learned in order to become a successful classroom manager she

A Remedy for Tardy Students

- Build a positive relationship so the student would rather be with you than elsewhere.
- The first five minutes of class time should be devoted to a review that's worth real points.
- Greet each student as they enter, providing the elements of human bonding.
- When a student is tardy, replace reprimands, threats, consequences, and punishment with a caring, concerned smile and the following statement: "I am glad you are here. I was getting worried about you."
- This is the way this should be handled even when the student is extremely late.
- Remember that the student is never allowed to make up the daily review assignment regardless of the value of the excuse.

Kids who continue to have problems with being late are indicating that something is going wrong in their lives and they need help solving the problem.

What doesn't work?

- Lectures, threats, and warnings.
- Detention, suspension, or incarceration.
- Consequences or rewards.
- Taking kids and parents to court.

A school is not a prison.

learned at her local McDonald's restaurant. "I noticed it was always the same. The hamburger was always the same thinness, it always had the same little onions on it, the 'secret sauce' still tasted the same, the employees always asked the same questions and dressed the same way."

What's the hallmark of all successful businesses? Predictability. People experience a predictable and good product delivered in the same way each and every time they come.

Predictability = Safety = Love

Is it true that our world is spinning faster and less predictably than ever before? As a result, are people… our students… drawn ever more toward anything that gives them a sense of order and safety? Ms. M. understood that doing the same thing at the beginning of each and every class was not only a gift of love to her students but also a gift to herself of fewer classroom hassles.

Little Things Make a Big Difference

Creating a calm and cooperative classroom culture sets the stage for successful classroom management. Once this foundation is formed, success involves doing a handful of very simple and small things consistently… rather than attempting to move mountains by constantly providing rewards or consequences.

KEEP YOUR HEAD ON A SWIVEL

As I watched Mark's teacher, Ms. Matsuoka, I was reminded of a neighbor of mine (Charles) who'd served in the Marines. Just about every weekend, he'd meander over to our yard and start up a conversation. "Situational awareness" was his thing. Such awareness had kept him alive in the jungles of Vietnam, so he figured it was worth keeping for a lifetime… and applying to every aspect of his life. George had situational awareness about the dandelions and moles in my yard and how they were sure to find their way into his. He had situational awareness about the strange cars visiting our row of mailboxes. He even had situational awareness about one of my roof shingles that seemed to be losing its seal. He was a great neighbor… as most potential problems got nipped in the bud before they grew wings. His signature farewell was, "Well… good talking to you. Keep your head on a swivel."

Some might have called him paranoid. I called him smart.

Jacob Kounin, as a result of his pioneering research in the 1970s, noticed something similar in highly effective classroom managers. Like Ms. M., they had uncanny situational awareness. They kept their head on a swivel, constantly scanning the environment for dandelions, moles, or loose shingles. Kounin and his colleagues called it "with-it-ness." As a result of this skill, master managers are able to identify misbehavior and address it before it grows. Less masterful classroom managers seem unaware of what's truly going on and fail to address problems until after they've become significant and widespread.

NIP IT IN THE BUD

I've tried ignoring the weeds in my garden, but it's never caused them to retreat. Pretending they don't exist has never stopped their photosynthesis. They still create chlorophyll and grow. Most of us have heard the adage: "Ignore it and it will go away." While it's true that overreacting to small problems will often make them worse, the same goes for completely ignoring them.

Ms. M.... and all of the great educators we've known... had an uncanny ability to sense when problems were developing and to address them before they grew. When I asked her about this, she said more or less the very same thing I'd heard from scores of other successful educators:

LOVE AND LOGIC EXPERIMENT:
The Problem Chair

TEACHER (with a calm whisper): "I have another chair for you right here. That chair you've been using has always been a problem."

STUDENT: "Geeze! I'm not doing anything wrong."

TEACHER (with a friendly grin): "I know. It's that chair. It's not your fault. This chair over by me is way better. Thanks."

STUDENT: "This is so dumb. Why should I have to move?"

TEACHER (walking away): "I agree. I think the custodian should take that chair out to the dumpster. It was a problem for a few students last year, too."

"I don't wait until I'm sure there's a problem. If I even get a sense... even a small inkling... that a student is getting restless or something is starting to happen... I find a way to get myself over to that part of the room. Because I always teach while walking, there's no harm done if I'm wrong... which often seems to be the case."

What's most likely true? Is it "A" or "B"?

A. Was she often wrong about disruptions beginning to develop?

B. Was she often correct, but the incipient disruptions were nipped in the bud because of her keen awareness and proximity?

The only downside of preventing misbehavior is that we never really know how much we've prevented.

USE QUICK AND EASY PREVENTATIVE INTERVENTIONS

True Love and Logic teachers challenge themselves each and every day: "I wonder how long I can go without having to provide a consequence for misbehavior?"

They don't grasp this challenge because they're permissive. No way! They do so because they understand that highly effective teachers prevent misbehavior while less effective ones constantly react to it. They also do so because they understand the following:

- When I have to stop to provide a consequence, I am no longer teaching.
- When I'm no longer teaching, other students get restless and begin to act out.
- Besides, I don't really have any consequences that will scare my toughest students into behaving.

In our observations of thousands of highly skilled classroom managers, we've discovered they mostly rely on a variety of subtle actions, all designed to redirect behavior while maintaining the flow of instruction. We call these *Quick and Easy Classroom Interventions*. Listed below are some examples:

- Smile at the student and wink, sending a nonverbal message, "Please stop."
- Move slowly toward the student, continuing to teach as you do.
- If the student responds well to touch, briefly and gently rest your hand on their shoulder as you teach.
- Use humor by whispering in their ear, "Will you save that for your teacher next hour? She likes that stuff."
- Confuse the student by whispering something like, "Tell me about your dog after class," and immediately resume the lesson.
- Slip a note to the student reading, "Just because I like you, should I allow you to keep doing that?"
- Ask the student to return some library books, talk to the custodian about the heat, take an envelope to the office, etc.
- Whisper to the student, "I'm concerned that you may get in trouble. Please walk with me as I teach." The student can simply follow you for a while as you work.
- Ask the student to help you by emptying the pencil sharpener, erasing the board, organizing books, etc.
- Ask the student a question about the lesson that will help them feel good about themselves.
- Whisper with a smile, "Will you stop that... just for me?" Then quickly return to the lesson after doing so.
- Quietly ask the student, "How can I help?"
- Ask the student, "Is this the right time and place for that behavior? Will you save that for recess (or after school)?"
- Ask the student to move to another location, emphasizing that this is intended to help them avoid getting into trouble.
- Whisper with empathy, "Oh... man... it looks like you're having a hard day. If you want to talk about it, let's set a time."

Keep on Trucking

Does it ever seem as if there are just two types of parents in every store? While this question may seem to have nothing to do with classroom behavior management, we think you'll begin to see its relevance.

Let's first consider Parent "A" who's just walked into the Family Interaction Research Lab (Walmart) with their four-year-old.

LITTLE LOUIE (whining like a loose fan belt): "What do I get if I'm good?"

MOTHER: "If you're really good I'll get you an ice cream cone."

LOUIE (throwing himself on the floor): "I don't want ice cream! I want a toy. It's been so long since I got anything new!"

MOTHER (kneeling on one knee, attempting to make some eye contact): "You already have so many toys. I'll get you a Coke. You can have a Coke if you are really good."

LOUIE (still writhing on the floor): "A toy! I want a toy!"

MOTHER (now on both knees)

Who is leading whom? Who's training whom?

Let's now consider Parent "B" who is two aisles away and moving near the speed of light toward the dairy section.

LITTLE LES (working hard to keep up with his dear mother): "What do I get if I'm good?"

MOTHER (rounding the end cap toward the milk): "A happy life."

LES (throwing himself on the floor): "But I want a…"

MOTHER (giving Les's protest zero airtime and roaring toward the produce aisle): "Try to keep up, and try not to get lost. It's always a better day when I get out of the store with the same number of kids I brought in."

Preventing and Minimizing Classroom Disruptions

When you think a student (or students) may be on the verge of acting up... → Move toward them.

But keep teaching as you do.

If they don't, experiment with something like:

Resting your hand gently on their shoulder.

Or...

Asking, "Will you save that for Mrs. Reyes's class next period?"

Or...

Sending them on a quick errand.

If they behave, move away from them.

Remember to immediately resume teaching as you briefly apply these very small and very quick "interventions." → Save consequences for the "big stuff."

Who's setting the tone? Who's leading whom? Who's in charge here?

As noted above, one of the primary behaviors of educators who struggle with classroom management is that they stop too frequently and for too long. Sometimes they stop to provide a reward. Sometimes they stop to have a far too lengthy discussion with a student about his or her behavior. Sometimes they stop to place a student's name on the board... or to take away points... or to perform some other duty required by the "classroom management" approach they are using.

Under these circumstances, who is leading whom? Who is training whom? Who's really in charge?

If students can get us to stop teaching, they will always get us to stop teaching.

In contrast, highly successful classroom managers apply quick and easy preventative interventions. As they go about each lesson, they continually remind themselves, "Keep on trucking." Throughout the pages of this book you've already seen the theme:

Teachers continue the lesson as they calmly approach the student. They whisper something to the student, immediately resume teaching and move toward another area of the classroom. In most cases they stop for no longer than ten to fifteen seconds.

SAVE THE CONSEQUENCES FOR THE BIG STUFF

A central tenet of many classroom management systems is the idea that every instance of misbehavior should receive an immediate consequence. The educators who suffer most are those who conscientiously attempt to meet this unrealistic and overwhelming demand.

One teacher described how she gradually came to realize that trying to provide consequences for everything was creating more chaos than good:

"I was taught in my behavior management classes that I had to provide a logical consequence every time a student misbehaved. As a young teacher I was ready and willing to meet this challenge. I'd carefully created a poster-sized chart with each student's name on it. Each day they started with a certain number of points. They could earn more points by doing positive things, and they could lose points for acting out or refusing to do their work. They could even use their points at the end of the week to earn special privileges or treats. I even laminated the chart. B.F. Skinner would have been proud.

"It soon became evident that there wasn't enough time in the day to both teach and to implement my behavior management system. Besides, it seemed as if many of my most challenging students constantly argued with me about their points or didn't care about the consequences or rewards they received. Something had to give!

"Instead of entirely giving up on the idea of providing consequences for every infraction, I set aside my point system and tried a more informal strategy. Each time a student acted up, I went to them and discussed what they might do to repay me for their poor choice. I even encouraged them to solve the problem rather than having me do something about their behavior. I thought I was using Love and Logic. As a result, I even badmouthed the approach to some of my peers, complaining that I still wasn't getting any teaching done.

"My true transformation began when I attended a *9 Essential Skills for the Love and Logic Classroom* training provided by our counselor. I still remember Jim Fay's words:

**'Save the consequences for the big stuff.
Use Quick and Easy Classroom Interventions
for the little stuff.'**

"Now I feel a lot freer to teach without having to make every problem a capital offense. The strange thing is, now that I'm not so worried about providing consequences for everything, my students are actually better behaved!"

CHAPTER EIGHT

Guiding Kids to Own and Solve Their Problems

It was the first day of our annual summer conference. I (Jim) stood at the door greeting the attendees. She shook my hand and said, "Hi, Jim, I'm Sally Ogden. I've been teaching for a while, and you know the sad thing? I graduated from college with a degree in education and no skills on how to manage the classroom!"

I was surprised by her candor. "The great thing about this conference," I replied, "is that everybody leaves at the end with lots of new classroom management experiments. When you start to hear them, you might even begin looking forward to the new school year... so you can try them out."

She grimaced, "Oh, I hope so. The stress has been horrible. I'm feeling like toast... so burned out. The crazy thing... the hardest thing... is that I was named Colorado Teacher of the Year, and I'm embarrassed that I have so few skills on dealing with discipline problems with my students."

I was at a loss for words.

Sally continued, "The truth is, Jim, I've heard great things about you. I don't want to put any pressure on you, but I'm relying on this conference to keep me from becoming so burned out that I have to change careers!"

I probably stammered something intelligent like, "Well… uh… no pressure… uh."

"I am hoping you can give me some new attitudes and techniques so I can teach for many more years, and have fun doing it." She shared, "I want to feel excited about it again… to keep the spirit."

I saw Sally several times during the conference and she seemed to be enjoying the presentations. She was a great student, asking quite a few in-depth questions and frequently putting me on the spot with, "But what do you do when a kid says _____?"

A Grimace Turned to a Smile

I saw Sally a year later. The slight grimace she wore the summer before was replaced by a relaxed, confident smile. "Jim, I've got to tell you! Teaching is fun again. I've had a blast this year!"

"Wow, Sally! What brought that on?"

"Jim, I did what you told me to do. I picked my favorite technique from last year's conference and I ran an experiment… and this is going to make you laugh."

"So which technique was it?" I inquired. "And what's so funny?"

"Oh, I chose that one called *Guiding Kids to Own and Solve Their Problems*. I teach middle school. There's always a huge amount of drama, and the kids are always looking to me to solve all of their woes. I'd try to help, but no matter what suggestions I gave them, they'd roll their eyes and say, 'like that won't work' or 'that's lame.' No matter how hard I worked, I always felt like a failure."

"Have you landed your helicopter?" I asked jokingly.

"No… it crashed," she laughed. "I had to find a

> **LOVE AND LOGIC EXPERIMENT:**
> ### Eye Rolling
>
> STUDENT: Rolls their eyes at something the teacher says.
>
> TEACHER (smiles, pauses, and speaks dramatically): "Can you see your brains when you do that?"

different form of transportation. Hovering over the kids and trying to rescue them from all of their problems was the source of my burn-out. Anyway, Jim, I had this eighth grade French class. Every Thursday we had an exercise that the kids called 'Room Objects Day.' Each would pick a partner and go around the room speaking in French, pointing out various objects, and asking each other to name them."

LOVE AND LOGIC EXPERIMENT:
I'm Gifted!

STUDENT: "I shouldn't have to memorize all this stuff. It's irrelevant, because I'm gifted."

TEACHER (with a grin): "Nice try..."

"So they'd take turns asking and answering in French?" I asked.

She nodded, "You got it. This rather socially challenged little guy named Winston always headed my way, whining that he didn't have a partner. In the past I'd try to rescue by finding him one. Then he'd whine even more about the person I found. The saga was as predictable as night and day, and it always burned up a huge amount of my time and energy. It became a weekly exercise in futility."

"This sounds so familiar," I interrupted. "It seems like every time we rescue someone from a problem they are capable of solving, they're never happy with the quality of our rescue. Then we're the bad guy. It's like, the more we try to be the hero, the more we end up being the villain."

"I think that's right, Jim. That's why I was always feeling worn out. Anyway, I decided to experiment with *Guiding Kids to Own and Solve Their Problems*. The next time he pursued me complaining he didn't have a partner, I surprised him by empathizing, 'That's such a bummer. Wow, that's hard.' Then I asked, 'Winston, what do you think you're going to do?'"

The rest of their conversation…

WINSTON (shrugging his shoulders and studying his shoes):
"I dunno."

SALLY: "Would you like to hear what some other kids have tried in situations like this?"

WINSTON: "Guess so."

SALLY: "Well… some kids just sit down and don't do anything. How would that work for you?"

Sally told me, "At that moment, I got the surprise of my life. My teaching world turned upside down. A major paradigm shift hit me. He answered, 'But, Mrs. Ogden, how am I supposed to learn anything?' That was the moment I realized something: All along I'd held the belief that kids really didn't want to learn, and that it was my job to make them do so. Winston just proved me wrong. What a paradigm shift! This hit me so hard that I must have just stared at him."

WINSTON (bringing Sally back to earth): "But what else? But what else? What am I supposed to do?"

SALLY: "Oh, I don't know. I guess some kids might find a twosome and make it into a threesome. How do you think that might work?"

WINSTON "We wouldn't get as many chances, so we wouldn't learn as much. What else?"

SALLY: "Gee, I don't know. I guess some kids would do it themselves. They would ask the question and then answer the question."

WINSTON "That's all you have?"

SALLY (with empathy): "I guess so. I've run out of ideas."

WINSTON (walking away and muttering to himself): 'That's stupid… won't work."

Sally confessed, "Jim, that was my first experiment with *Guiding Kids to Own and Solve Their Problems*, and I didn't like how it left me feeling. I felt like I was letting Winston down right at a time when he needed me. I'd always believed it was a teacher's job to solve problems for kids, even though I'd heard you say that teaching kids to solve problems involves a higher level of love. The only thing that kept me from telling Winston how to solve his problem right on the spot was a statement you made during last summer's conference. You said, 'When we solve a problem a child is capable of solving, we meet our needs. When we guide them to own and solve these problems, we meet theirs.'"

I nodded, "That's right. When we solve problems for others it feels good. There's nothing wrong with that… except when we become more concerned with feeling good than helping kids see that they are capable."

Sally went on to say that five minutes later, Winston was going around the room, pointing at room objects asking himself, "Qu'est que c'est?" and answering himself, "C'est une lumière… C'est un bureau…"

She continued, "I couldn't believe it! If I'd told him to do something like that, he'd never have done it. Somehow suggesting, 'Some students decide to' made all the difference in the world."

"Nobody likes to be told what to do," I agreed. "It's always more effective to use, 'Some students decide to' or 'Some people decide to.'"

"I haven't told you the best part, Jim!"

Sally described what happened the following week during their room objects activity:

Winston (approaching Mrs. Ogden with a forlorn, "lost puppy" look): "Guess what, Mrs. Ogden?"
Sally (doing her best to be empathetic): "Oh, I bet you don't have a partner. That's a real bummer. What do you think you are going to do?"

Winston: "I don't know what I'm going to do, but I know what I'm not going to do… not doing twice as much work like last time!"

Doesn't that sound like a typical eighth grade kid who hates the fact that he had to do more work than any of the others? Needless to say, Sally was hooked on Love and Logic.

Let's take a closer look at the process used by Mrs. Ogden with Winston.

Guiding Kids to Own and Solve Their Problems

Step One: Provide a sincere dose of empathy.

As we know, empathy opens the heart and the mind to learning.

Step Two: Ask, "What do you think you are going to do?"

Asking this question gently, yet firmly, places the problem on their shoulders to solve. It also sends a powerful unstated message of confidence: "I believe in you! I know you have what it takes to overcome this challenge."

Very rarely… if ever… do kids respond to this question by describing some wise strategy for solving their problem. More often, they react by shrugging their shoulders and mumbling, "I don't know." Some students even reply, "I'm telling you. That's what I'm doing to solve this." Obviously, this is a telltale sign that the student in question has spent most of their life around adults who rescue.

Step Three: Ask, "Would you like to hear what some students have tried?"

As Sally Ogden discovered with Winston, students are far more likely to listen when we describe what "some other students" have tried, rather than telling them what they could or should do.

"Would you like to hear what some students have tried?" is a sincere question. If the student says "no" we respect their desire.

Of course, we leave the door open by replying, "If you change your mind, please let me know."

If the student replies in the affirmative, move to step four.

STEP FOUR: Provide two or three options, after each one, asking, "How will that work for you?"
"Easier said than done!" commented one rather blunt educator. "When a kid says 'yes,' I usually can't think of a single thing to suggest."

When this happens, it's perfectly fine… in fact, great… if we admit it to the student: "I'm going to have to give some more thought to this. What if I think about it and you think about it, and we visit tomorrow?" Obviously, this buys us time to think and to visit with others for ideas. There's another benefit: By the time tomorrow rolls around, we often discover that the child has either already solved the problem or decided it wasn't a problem to begin with."

Some educators decide to develop a readymade list of possible options for solving the problems students bring to them most frequently.

Common problems students bring my way:

- **"You didn't explain it."** (The student lacks information because they were either physically or mentally absent when you provided it.)
- **"I don't have a pencil."** (Or book, laptop, tablet, paper, etc.)
- **"He called me a _____."**
- **"You need to give me another chance. I need to pass this class!"** (Upset about their grade.)
- **"Nobody likes me."**
- **The student has caused a problem for others and now needs to solve it.**

After creating a list like the one above, some teachers decide to brainstorm with their friends two or three possible options they can give students each time these "high frequency" issues come up. Before this chapter ends, we'll give you a few quick ones.

It's also important to remember it's not our job to provide brilliant options. Our role is not to solve the problem, it's to help the student see a process for solving the problem. We want kids to realize that problems are most effectively solved through a process of brainstorming, evaluating the potential merits of possible remedies, and experimentation. We don't want them to believe that solving problems is reliant on one being brilliant enough to conjure up quick and magical fixes. Those who believe in the former are likely to persevere. Those who adhere to the latter quickly give up when difficulties arise.

Love and Logic is all about helping young people develop a healthy understanding of cause and effect. I (Charles) want kids to have enough of this precious commodity between their ears, that when they are teens or adults, they don't need warning labels on their coffee to know something tragic might happen if they drive around town holding a scalding beverage between their legs. Is it just me, or does it also seem to you that fewer and fewer people have the basic notion that $1 + 2$ might equal 3?

One of the ways we help students develop this mental, cause-and-effect math is by asking, "How will that work for you?" after providing each option:

Some students decide to_____. How will that work for you?

Others decide to_____. How will that work for you?

Wise Love and Logic parents and educators are so deeply devoted to the concept of helping children develop cause and effect that they usually provide a rather lousy option first. This provides practice for the prefrontal, "What might happen if I _____?" cortex, and it also leaves the student feeling smart. There's an added benefit of starting with a less-than-stellar idea: Kids tend to reject the first thing we offer, so when they do, we haven't wasted a really good one.

STEP FIVE: End with, "I wish you success with this. Please let me know how it works out."

We used to teach people to end this process with, "Good luck. Let me know how this works out." We no longer do so for two important reasons: First, very few people are able to say this without sounding sarcastic or flippant. Secondly, we've become concerned about young people believing that "luck" is the key to success. Successful people know it's not about the roll of the dice but about hard work and perseverance.

As we prepare to send the student off to own and solve their problem, many of us struggle with the temptation to tell them which solution to try. Don't make this mistake. When we say, "I really think the third idea is the best" or "Try the third one we talked about" we steal from the student. If all goes well, we steal their chance to feel great about making the choice. If things go poorly, we steal their opportunity to take personal responsibility for the choice and to learn from it.

There are certainly times when we cringe a bit as the student goes off prepared to use an option we believe is sure to fail. There's no doubt that sometimes we simply have to step in and say, "No." When serious issues come up, we have an obligation to protect our students from themselves and others. Nevertheless, we absolutely must allow them to learn from their poor decisions... so they have the commonsense problem-solving skills essential for

> **LOVE AND LOGIC EXPERIMENT:**
> ## No Friends
>
> STUDENT: "I don't have any friends."
>
> TEACHER: "That's really sad. What do you think you're going to do?"
>
> STUDENT: "I don't know."
>
> TEACHER: "Would you like to hear what some other kids have tried?"

leading safe and healthy lives. The Love and Logic mantra is always the same: Hope and pray they make plenty of mistakes when the stakes are relatively low, so they won't have to make them when the stakes are life and death.

Guiding Kids to Solve Their Own Problems

Step 1. Empathy.

"How sad. I bet that makes you unhappy."

Step 2. Hand the problem back to the student.

"What do you think you're going to do?"

Step 3. Offer choices.

"Would you like to hear what other kids have tried?"

Step 4. Have the student state the consequences.

"And how will that work?"

Step 5. Give permission for the student to either solve the problem or not solve the problem.

"I wish you success with this. Please let me know how it works out."

Identify Some Readymade Options

As we admitted earlier, it's not always easy to think of options we can provide to students after we've asked, "Would you like to hear what some students decide to try?" That's why we suggest identifying the most common problems students present, as well as some readymade options you can provide each and every time these issues arise. Listed below are some examples:

> **"You didn't explain it."** (The student lacks information because they were either physically or mentally absent when you provided it.) Some students decide to...
> - say to themselves, "Well... this project isn't that important so I'll just ignore it."
> - stay after school so that they can visit with me when I have some time to talk.

- talk with another student and see if they can explain it to them.

"I don't have a pencil." (Or book, laptop, tablet, paper, etc.)
Some students decide to…
- try to complete the assignment in their head and then get it down on paper as soon as they have a chance.
- see if they can find someone who will lend them one.
- ask a friend if they will share.

"He called me a _____."
Some students decide to…
- let this ruin their day.
- smile at the other student and confuse them by saying, "Thanks, I appreciate your honest feedback." Then walk away quickly.
- remember that kids usually say things like that because they are feeling really low about themselves.

"You need to give me another chance. I need to pass this class!" (Upset about their grade.)
Some students decide to…
- do some research on summer school options.
- sit closer to the teacher so they aren't so distracted by their friends.
- get some tutoring.

"Nobody likes me."
Some students decide to…
- tell some other kids that they need to be their friend.
- once in a while notice nice and special things about some of the other kids in class. For example, "I noticed that you like to draw horses." Then they listen and make the other person feel special.
- find another kid who doesn't have a friend and make friends with him or her.

The student has caused a problem for others and now needs to solve it.

Some students decide to…

- let their teacher solve the problem and experience the consequences. Personally, I'm not thinking I would go for that one. Around here it's usually a lot more pleasant for students when they solve problems than when they let their teachers solve them.
- write a plan for what they are going to do differently and discuss it with their teacher when it's convenient for her. That would probably be before school, after school, or during lunch or recess.
- do some helpful things to put energy back into their teacher. If you are interested, I can share some ideas.

"What an Energy Drain."

As you surely remember, students in a Love and Logic classroom may do anything they like… as long as it doesn't cause a problem for anyone else in the universe. Thirteen-year-old Ezra had decided to test just how far he could go before his wonderful teacher, Mr. Sakda, informed him that his actions were qualified as problematic.

Some educators prefer to create rigid systems where students have few choices, experience little freedom, are spoon-fed solutions to every issue, and constantly experience the enticement of tangible rewards. Love and Logic educators rise to a higher calling. They yearn to help students develop the self-control and problem-solving skills learned only when students have opportunities to err. The payoff can be massively gratifying!

MR. SAKDA (with wonderful empathy): "Oh… man… Ezra… you really caused a problem yesterday when you kept getting out of your seat and were messing with other kids."

EZRA: "I just had to sharpen my pencil."

MR. SAKDA: "I didn't want to embarrass you in front of the class, so I decided to visit with you today when I could do it quietly. That really drained my energy. What are you going to do to replace it?"

When you can't think of a consequence, have an energy drain.

Have you ever found yourself at a total and complete loss for a natural or logical consequence? The next time this happens, experiment with having an energy drain. The *Energy Drain* is an actual certified and time-tested Love and Logic technique. Just remember: When you can't think of a consequence, have an energy drain. Here are the steps:

STEP ONE: Inform the student that their behavior has drained your energy.

This sounds like, "Oh… no… When you_____, it really drained my energy."

The nice thing about misbehavior is that it does drain our energy. This being the case, we are not speaking falsely when we say, "Oh… when you keep tapping on your desk when I try to teach, it really drains my energy."

STEP TWO: Ask, "How are you going to put that energy back into me (or the class/school)?"

If you're thinking, "Hey, this sounds a bit like restitution!" you nailed it. While there are times when we have to impose consequences, we prefer to guide students toward solving the problems they create. When we provide consequences, we have to do most of the thinking. When students are required to find ways to replace sapped energy, they have to do the thinking.

STEP THREE: Apply "Guiding Students to Own and Solve Their Problems."

Many educators find it extremely helpful to create a list of convenient "energy replacement options" for their classroom. When a student needs ideas, they can pick one, two, or more, depending on the severity of their draining behavior. Below is an excerpt from one developed by a wonderful middle school science teacher, Mrs. Carol Gwynn. The key is not to use her list, but to create one that fits your grade level and your unique classroom.

Mrs. Gwynn's Energy Replacement List

Scour, wash, and dry sinks and faucets.

Pick up litter from the floor.

Damp-dust windowsills and whiteboard tray.

Wash and dry the white laminated sheets at the front of the room.

Clean whiteboard.

Scrub, wash, and dry rectangular lab trays.

Count, sort, and clean specified lab equipment.

Damp-dust lab tray counter and splashboard.

Damp-dust room counters and bookshelves.

Damp-dust top of grow cabinet.

Remove plants from grow cabinet, clean inner walls, and replace plants.

Remove triple-beam balances, wash and dry each pan, placing it on its own balance, all posits on zero.

Organize compound microscopes: low power, body tube down, cord securely wrapped.

Organize stereoscope microscopes: low power, body tube down, cord securely wrapped.

Repair/replace dust covers on all microscopes.

Fill paper towel dispensers.

Empty pencil sharpener and damp dust sharpener area.

Wash windows.

Plaster holes in walls.

Check under all tables, remove gum, and repeat with chairs.

Square-up table (see circle on floor) and align chairs.

Water plants in, and on top of, cabinet.

Clean and polish the outside glass of aquaria and terraria.

Organize "Lost-and-Lonely" area.

Return books to appropriate classrooms.

Alphabetize student papers by last name.

Last school day of the week: remove last week's "Bonus Question & Answer," move this week's question down and add this week's answer. Select a new bonus question for next week.

Let's return to Ezra and Mr. Sakda.

MR. SAKDA: "That really drained my energy. What are you going to do to replace it?"

EZRA: "Huh? What are you talking about?"

MR. SAKDA: "Would you like to hear what some other students have done to replace energy in my class?"

EZRA: "What?"

MR. SAKDA: "Some students decide to ignore all of this and let their teacher do something about it. How would that work?"

EZRA: "Well, I didn't do anything wrong."

MR. SAKDA: "Personally, I don't think I'd let the teacher do something. Usually when I have to solve problems for kids, it goes a lot worse for them than when they do it for themselves. But... I guess you have to decide about such things."

EZRA: "What am I supposed to do?"

MR. SAKDA (turning to leave): "Oh... look at the time. I need to run. We can visit tomorrow."

Is This Practical for a Busy Teacher?

Some educators wonder, "How do I provide all of this guidance when I hardly have a minute to spare during the day?"

The answer to this question is twofold: First, this process should require very little time on the part of the teacher. Remember, it's not our job to provide an endless list of solutions or to spend extended time processing each and every option provided. Our objective is to hand the problem back, to offer two or three possible ideas, and to move on with life.

Secondly, this process is often the most effective when we don't try to do it in one sitting with the student. Let's see how Mr. Sakda applies this process on his time and terms rather than Ezra's.

EZRA: "Yeah, but you said you had some ideas."

MR. SAKDA: "I do. We'll visit tomorrow."

The next day:

MR. SAKDA: "Do you have any ideas about how you are going to replace my energy?"

EZRA: "You said you had some ideas."

MR. SAKDA: "I do. Here's a list of some things you might do. I need to get started with class; we can visit later today or tomorrow."

The example of Mr. Sakda and Ezra is a true story shared by an educator who fell in love with the idea of getting his students thinking harder about their problems than he was. Apparently Ezra chose to help Mr. Sakda grade papers during lunch. What this involved was Ezra bringing his lunch to Mr. Sakda's room, eating with Mr. Sakda, and handing him ungraded papers one at a time. Over three consecutive days, the two ate together and worked together. During this time, Mr. Sakda didn't lecture and didn't act perturbed in any way. Quite the contrary, he frequently commented about how thankful he was to have the help. On the second day, this wise teacher asked, "Do you have a dog? I have one. He is so naughty. He ate one of my shoes." Ezra had a dog, too. Unlike his teacher's, his was well-behaved.

Mr. Sakda commented:

"In a weird way, I felt a bit guilty about handling it this way. It was almost like I felt bad about not lecturing or being stern or trying to make the whole thing into a capital offense. I felt more unsure when this kid seemed to enjoy helping.

"The following week, another student was creating a bit of a disruption. On the way out of class, Ezra whispered to me, 'Hey... Mr. Sakda, is that kid draining your energy? I

could come by and help you get some back if you want me to.'

"I almost cried right there. I shouldn't have been surprised. I'd seen it before. Most kids really do want to connect with us and to repair the problems they create."

All Ages Can Benefit

Sally Ogden, amazed by her success with *Guiding Kids to Own and Solve Their Problems*, became a vocal advocate of using the approach with young teens. She was often heard saying, "This was made for middle school students." Then she was transferred to the high school. Since her new students were older, are you guessing she found no use for this process, or did she discover that it came in handy multiple times daily? Like almost all Love and Logic strategies, this one applies from early childhood to geriatric settings.

One of her favorite stories is about Sara who came to her in a frantic way saying, "Look at this report card! I can't take this home! My parents are going to freak! I'll be grounded forever! They'll take away my learner's permit! What am I supposed to do?"

Here was another situation where a student's problem could soon become the teacher's problem. Sally's job was to gently hand this problem back to Sara. She reminded herself, "The purpose of this technique is to teach kids to think about options and to help them learn that they can, in fact, solve problems for themselves."

Starting with empathy, Sally said, "Wow. That's got to be terrifying. What do you think you are going to do?"

"How should I know? I've never even gotten grades like this before. My parents are going to kill me!"

"Would you like to hear what some other kids have tried?"

"I guess so. I just can't show my parents this report card."

Sally continued, "I can't think of anything right off the top of my head. I'll think real hard about it, and if you come back right after school, maybe I can have a list of options."

Sara came into Sally's room after school with high expectations written all over her face. "Mrs. Ogden. I hope you have some ideas, 'cause my parents are going to freak."

Sally started with the worst possible option. "Well, Sara, some kids just lie to their parents telling them the school has a new policy and doesn't give report cards anymore. How do you think that would work?"

"Oh, that'll never fly with my parents. They're too smart for that. Besides, they'd just call the principal to check and then I'd really be in trouble."

Before we continue with this example, let's consider how we might respond to a student who says, "Oh... lying about it... that sounds like a good idea." Wise educators understand that telling students what they should or shouldn't do increases the odds of rebellion. So does lecturing students about the consequences of various choices. Aware of this, effective teachers describe their concerns about what might happen if they, themselves, made the poor choice. By taking this approach, we can plant seeds about cause and effect without entering a control battle nobody can win.

TEACHER: "Oh... I'd worry that if I lied to my parents, they'd find out and I'd be in even bigger trouble. And, I guess that I'd worry about feeling really guilty about being so deceptive."

STUDENT: "I wouldn't worry about that."

TEACHER: "And do you think I'd have to tell your parents the truth if they asked me about your grade?"

Establishing the fact that we don't condone lying or doing anything else that's hurtful, let's get back to Mrs. Ogden's example.

"Well, let's see," Sally continued. "I've known some kids who had their friends change the grades on the report card. Then if your parents asked if you changed the grade, you could honestly tell them that you didn't change them. How do you think that might work?"

"No way!" Sara complained. "My dad's just like a detective. He'll sniff that out in a hurry... then he'll really be on my case. Don't you have any other ideas? These are lame!"

"Well," Sally replied, "I'm running out of ideas, but I guess some students would just go home, tell the truth, and admit to getting lazy. They'd say that they really learned their lesson and promise to bring the grade up before the end of the grading period. They'd probably lay it on pretty thick about how sorry they were and beg for their parents to understand. How do you think that might work?"

It was clear Sara was not thrilled by the option. "Mrs. Ogden, you could call them for me and tell them to go easy on me and that they shouldn't take my learner's permit."

With a caring smile, Sally answered, "Yes, Sara, I could do that, but tell me something. Who believes you are strong enough to handle this on your own?"

Sara studied the floor. "I guess you do."

"That's right, Sara, I wish you the best. Let me know how it works out."

Bright and early the next morning Sara burst into Mrs. Ogden's room. She was beaming.

"Guess what, Mrs. Ogden? You should have seen me last night! I was so good! I blew my parents away! They couldn't even handle me!"

"How's that, Sara?"

"I took that report card home and threw it down on the table. Then I yelled, 'Look at that lousy report card! Boy, did I learn my lesson. I'm really going to have to knuckle down!'"

Sally was speechless.

Sara continued, "I know my dad doesn't like to be told what to do, so I put my finger right in his face and told him that he'd better do something about this! He was so blown away he didn't do anything. I'm so good!"

And with that, Sara raced out of the room with her friends.

You may know Sally Ogden. She went on to teach many more years and became one of America's most entertaining public speakers. She is the author of many books and materials, two of our favorites being: *No Thanks, I Just Had a Banana!* and *Words will NEVER Hurt Me.*

We like to think of *Guiding Kids to Own and Solve Their Problems* as a no-lose technique. If a youngster picks a bad option, real world learning takes place. If he selects a good one, he enjoys a wonderful opportunity to feel great about himself. Consider the following example provided to us by a second grade teacher, Mrs. Hicks:

BRAYDEN: "Mrs. Hicks! Landon and those guys won't let me play soccer during recess. It's not fair!"

MRS. HICKS: "Brayden. That's really sad. What do you think you are going to do about that?"

BRAYDEN: "I dunno."

MRS. HICKS: "Would you like to hear what some other kids have tried?"

BRAYDEN (pouting): "No. Just go tell those kids to let me play."

MRS. HICKS: "Well, I could do that, but I'm afraid it might make things worse for you."

BRAYDEN: "Why? You could just tell them to let me play."

MRS. HICKS: "They might start calling you 'teacher's pet,' and I bet you might know how bad that can get."

BRAYDEN: "Okay, so what have other kids tried?"

MRS. HICKS: "Some kids just decide to feel bad and don't do anything about it. How would that work out?"

BRAYDEN (eyes wide with shock): "But that's no good!"

MRS. HICKS: "Well, I guess some kids would find something

	else to play. How would that work out?"
BRAYDEN:	"But I want to play soccer!"
MRS. HICKS:	"I only have one more idea. Some kids decide to make friends with Landon. They share their candy with him and do stuff like that. How do you think that would work?"
BRAYDEN:	"I dunno."
MRS. HICKS:	"Brayden, those are the ideas I have. Maybe you can think up some other ones that are better. I wish you success with this. Please let me know how it works out for you."

A Lifetime Gift

Is it Mrs. Hicks's job to keep offering new ideas until Brayden finds one he likes? Of course not. It's her job to get him thinking and realizing he can solve the problems he faces. A solution from another person is a one-time event. Learning to think and solve problems is a gift that lasts a lifetime.

> *A solution from another person is a one-time event. Learning to think and solve problems is a gift that lasts a lifetime.*

Let's suppose Brayden chooses a bad option. Will this be a great opportunity for him to learn when the "price tag" of learning such lessons is still small? Is it true that the road to wisdom is paved with mistakes?

What if he makes a great choice? Will this result in great satisfaction and feelings of confidence? Once again, it's a no-lose proposition.

Apparently Brayden ignored all of Mrs. Hicks's advice and decided to form a "virtual" soccer training camp, where he and some of his more creative... albeit a bit odd... buddies ran around practicing moves without a ball. Mrs. Hicks admitted,

"I never could have come up with such a bad option that he would have liked so much." It just shows that the best solution to every person's problem usually resides within the skin of that person.

The Earlier the Better

When my (Charles's) wife, Monica, and I realized we were having a later-in-life impromptu blessing child, we decided we'd begin as early as possible with *Guiding Kids to Own and Solve Their Problems*. By the time our son Cody was four, he'd been on the receiving end of it so many times he'd become an expert.

Then it happened. Monica was struggling with her computer. It wasn't behaving.

Cody arrived on the scene. "What's wrong, Mommy?"

Venting a bit, she explained, "This thing is all locked up. The mouse won't even work. I've been hassling with this for an hour."

Without missing a beat, he replied, "That is so sad, Mommy. What are you gonna do? Would you like to hear what other mommies do with their computers?"

More than a bit amused, she replied, "Sure!"

Grinning from ear to ear and giggling, he advised, "Some mommies run over it with their bike. How would that work out, Mommy?"

Mom was too stunned to produce sound.

Cody's face turned more serious. "But other mommies shut off their computers and go out in the yard and play with me and let the computer fix itself. How would that work?"

A proud mother shut off the computer, went out to play with Cody, and what do you know? That universal computer fix actually worked. When she booted it up, it worked!

Today's kids are going to live in a world that is even more complex than the one we know today. There will be more tough decisions to make and more problems to solve. There's no way we can change that world to fit our kids. Our job is to help them learn to face the world they will enter. That's why... more than ever before... they need plenty of practice owning and solving their problems.

CHAPTER NINE

Reaching Your Unmotivated Students

Trips

Ashton had spent the previous nine years of school developing a finely honed, highly sophisticated network of avoidance skills. Most of these coping skills involved taking trips: trips to the pencil sharpener… trips to the school nurse to address vague, yet reoccurring physiological afflictions… trips to the principal's office for predictable lectures about how rough his life would be if he didn't get an education… trips to the teacher's desk to discuss perceived maltreatment by peers… trips to other galaxies where school didn't exist… trips… trips… trips.

Perhaps you know a student like Ashton. Each year for about four decades we've asked educators, "What's the biggest challenge you face with students?" They've consistently replied, "Capable kids who won't do their work."

There's good news. There's hope. While there's no silver bullet, quick-fix solution to chronic underachievement, there are strategies that can keep us out of endless power struggles while helping students view learning as rewarding. Wise educators understand the process of improvement for these students is often very slow. With some, it may take months or even years for them to shed their psychological armor and take the risks required to achieve at their highest potential. I (Charles) was one of those students. Because of undiagnosed learning problems and illnesses, I found myself as a young student struggling and growing more and more reluctant to try. I thank all of the wonderful teachers who looked past my obstinate… often obnoxious… behavior to see the scared and discouraged kid within. Without them… and my wonderfully patient parents… I would have never experienced the joy of learning and achievement.

This Should Have Worked

Mrs. Karen Freeman and the team at Yates Academy Middle School were as skilled and caring as they come. Dedicated to ensuring that all students learned and achieved at high levels, they were confident they'd be successful in their efforts to help Ashton become more excited about achievement.

Their first step involved conducting a thorough assessment of Ashton's academic strengths and weaknesses. Dr. Lambert, their

LOVE AND LOGIC EXPERIMENT:
Why Do We Have To Do This?

STUDENT: "I don't know why we have to learn this. I'm never going to need this when I get out of here."

TEACHER (sincerely): "What do you dream of being when you are an adult?"

STUDENT: "Well… not somebody who has to do math all day."

TEACHER: "I hope that I can help you discover what you love to do… so that some day you can make it into a good career."

STUDENT: "Uh… well… football."

TEACHER: "That would be great. Will you work on that math… just for me… even though you really dislike it? Thanks! (Teacher walks away and attends to another student.)

well-trained school psychologist, administered an assortment of psychometrically reliable and valid aptitude and achievement measures. Before they were scored, she knew the results: Because Ashton was apathetic and passive resistant during the assessment process, she had no idea how capable or skilled he really was.

This was a good idea. It should have worked.

Undeterred by this minor setback, the Yates team developed a behavior system where Ashton could earn rewards for completing his work. This system also involved a home-school report system so Ashton's parents could participate by providing rewards at home. Because this system was based on solid research in behavioral psychology, and because it had worked with other students in the past, the team wasn't surprised when Ashton began to complete some assignments. What astonished them was how briefly the system worked. It wasn't long before Ashton had even become apathetic about earning rewards. This was a reasonable idea.

This was a good idea. It should have worked.

Mrs. Freeman and her team were not about to let a couple of bumps in the road get in the way of helping this wonderful kid. As such, they hypothesized, "Perhaps he is reluctant to try because of academic skill gaps and lack of confidence." This had often been the case with other students, so Ashton was provided one-on-one tutoring with a highly skilled academic intervention specialist. As the old adage goes, "You can lead a horse to water, but you can't make them drink." Ashton wasn't thirsty.

This also was a good idea. It should have worked.

Mr. Hamlin, the history teacher and football coach has remained quiet until this point. "I think he needs a kick in the butt," he suggested.

The rest of the team appeared rather shocked, even though most of them were thinking the same thing. Ever the class act, Mrs. Freeman asked, "In what sense are you talking? Would that be a literal kick or a figurative one?"

Hamlin chuckled. "Oh… a figurative one, of course. There needs to be some consequences for not doing his work. I agree that rewards and tutoring were the best place to start, but I think this kid needs some accountability."

"Well," replied Dr. Lambert, "I guess nothing else has worked."

The rest of the team reluctantly agreed, and they developed a system for using in-school suspension and restricting Ashton from participating in extracurricular activities such as football. Mrs. Freeman even set up a plan with Ashton's parents, so they could be part of the accountability team. The entire team even agreed that such consequences would only be effective if delivered with sincere empathy. Because this approach had helped some students in the past, there were high hopes it would assist Ashton. Can you imagine their frustration when it didn't? Ashton, remaining exceptionally apathetic, mumbled, "I don't care if you consequence me. Football isn't much fun anyway."

This had never really worked well with students like this in the past… but they were desperate.

Have you ever tried everything that makes sense with an apathetic student, just to find that nothing worked… or worked for very long? Students suffering from chronic, deep-seated motivational problems need a more chronic, deep-seated approach. They need one that gets below the surface to the foundation of their apathy. They need educators who are willing to apply slow and lasting solutions rather than quick fixes focused only on behavior, test scores, and grades.

The Roots of Chronic Academic Underachievement

A few summers ago, my (Charles's) apple tree stopped growing apples. The leaves started falling off, and some of the bark started to peel. One of the extremely helpful people at my local hardware store suggested that I water it more. Colorado is a dry place, so I figured, "That makes sense."

The next spring, fewer leaves appeared and more bark began to peel. "It's got to be insects," I reasoned, quickly applying a liberal coat of insecticide. As the summer arrived, no apples did either. This should have worked. It made sense.

Another spring and summer arrived. There were zero leaves, zero apples, and plenty of dead and peeling bark. Rather desperate, I reasoned, "Maybe if I prune it down it will resurrect itself. I've seen trees do that in the past." I cut away. While an extreme measure, it did make some sense.

This spring my poor apple tree began to tilt. When gravity finally pulled it to the ground, I discovered the culprit. I bet you guessed it. Something had attacked the roots. Studying the phenomenon, albeit a bit too late, I discovered the true cause of death: A soil born fungi with the fun name phytophthora root rot. From this postmortem analysis, I was reminded of a fundamental law of human behavior:

We won't see the fruit if we don't get to the roots.

Understanding the roots of academic apathy requires that we first understand the basics of intrinsic achievement motivation. One of my (Charles's) sons provided a powerful object lesson. As a toddler, less than two years old, Marc was extremely motivated to explore every nook and cranny of our home and to touch everything he could find… particularly those things being the most fragile or the most likely to cause serious injury or death. As young parents, we conscientiously applied Love and Logic. We also installed childproof latches on the cabinets containing hazardous materials.

All was right with the world. That is until the day he discovered he could unlock those cabinets by pulling them open until they stopped… then fishing around in the opening with a piece of track from his wooden train set.

The joy on his face was intense… like the one kids get when handed an ice cream cone. The look on my face was probably a lot different… like a child's whose cone had just plopped on the sidewalk.

What's this example tell us about intrinsic achievement motivation? We're all *born with* the following:

An intense drive to learn, explore, and master our environment.

Countless studies have confirmed our inborn, neurologically based need to achieve. Any time spent with a very young child confirms this fact. Little ones love to explore, love to manipulate the environment, and absolutely adore asking, "Why, why, why, why?"

The look on Marc's face illustrated another thing we are born with:

A strong neurochemical system for rewarding achievement.

What does it feel like to encounter obstacles, struggle, and eventually overcome them? Is there any greater feeling than the one we experience as a result of hard-earned mastery? On a neurochemical level, the brain responds to such experience with natural feel-good substances, not unlike those found in highly addictive drugs.

Working in tandem, the drive to learn and the built-in reward system provide the potential for high levels of achievement and a passion for lifelong learning. If this is the case, however, why are we as educators witnessing an epidemic of young people who seem almost compulsively motivated to avoid academic growth? Why are there so many Ashtons who fail to respond to strategies that should have worked?

The Root Causes of Underachievement

Five o'clock AM is not typically when I (Charles) find myself contemplating life's great mysteries. One January morning was different. It was unique because I found myself rushing out of the house to catch my way-too-early flight out of Denver International Airport. From my work as a teen waiter at a prestigious pancake house and late-night detox center, I learned the economy of carrying everything in one trip. There I was, trudging across my very dark and very cold driveway: suitcase in one hand… briefcase and coffee in the other… papers under my left arm… bagel tucked around my right pinkie finger.

I found it. Somehow I discovered the one small section of black ice remaining on the pavement. Who needs skis when they can achieve the same result with a much less expensive pair of dress shoes?

From experience, I've learned that falling doesn't hurt, but landing does. Heading toward the blacktop, I glimpsed something wonderful: the door handle of the car. Flailing about in utter desperation, I managed to grab it and keep myself upright. My cases were lying in the snow, my dog was eating my bagel, and I was wearing coffee. Nonetheless, I was upright.

At this point, you may be wondering, "What does Charles slipping on ice in his driveway have to do with my underachieving students?"

QUESTION: Is the brain exceptionally good at multitasking when physical or emotional survival is at stake?

ANSWER: No. When physical or emotional survival is threatened, the brain prioritizes. Portions of the cortex devoted to high-order learning and creativity are suppressed. Those devoted to survival are stimulated. Most of us know this as "fight or flight."

When basic needs are unmet, the brain filters out all information that is not directly relevant to meeting those needs.

QUESTION: What happens to the brain's drive to learn, and its built-in reward system, when more basic needs are unmet?

ANSWER: These two systems take a backseat to the brain's drive for basic survival.

QUESTION: What was the only thing I could think about and see as I was slipping on the ice?

ANSWER: Because it represented my only means of survival, the door handle of my car took precedence over everything else... even my coffee!

Do you have any students who are chronically "slipping on the ice?" Are these students unmotivated, or are they highly motivated by needs other than learning and academic achievement?

What Basic Needs Are Not Being Met In This Student's Life?

☐ Physical health and safety
☐ Unconditional love or acceptance
☐ Emotional safety
☐ Limits or boundaries
☐ Predictability
☐ Healthy control
☐ A sense of competence
☐ A sense of being needed by a group
☐ Hope

Rachel lives in a car with her younger sisters, her older brother, and her mentally ill mother. She never knows where they will park for the night, whether they'll have anything to eat, how cold she'll be, or how angry or pleasant her mother will act. Which of the following basic needs are not being met in Rachel's life?

- Physical health and safety
- Mental health and safety
- Unconditional love
- Structure, predictability, and limits
- A healthy sense of control
- Being a valued and needed member of a group
- Awareness that personal effort can lead to achievement

Carlton looks like all of his needs are met. He drives a new sports car to high school, lives in a nice home, and never has to worry about having enough to eat. His parents grew up in difficult economic and familial circumstances. They'd worked their fingers to the bone building an extremely successful business. Now their goal is to ensure Carlton never faces the disappointments or struggles that they did. As such, Carlton has never experienced a real limit or had to earn anything. He lives like a guest at a five-star resort.

Carlton is blessed that he doesn't face the severe deprivation suffered by Rachel. Nonetheless, he lacks much of what he truly needs to feel loved, emotionally safe, and capable of meeting life's challenges. Without limits, without chores, without accountability, and without purpose, many youth wallow in apathy.

James's parents have taken every Love and Logic parenting course they could. While far from perfect, they conscientiously do their best to provide good and loving, commonsense parenting. James, nevertheless, had started school on a rough note, quickly seeing that most of the other kids learned faster than he did. When he applies himself, he can learn at high levels, but he spends way too much time avoiding work. Are any of the basic needs not consistently met for James?

Many underachieving students are like James. They come from basically healthy life circumstances and have good teachers. Nevertheless, their learning problems leave them without a healthy sense of competency.

Some Solutions

The possible scenarios are endless. Underachieving students enter our classrooms from every conceivable walk of life. Some come from poverty. Others come from wealth. Some have parents with mental health issues, addictions, or other serious problems. Others don't. Some are neglected. Others are overindulged. Some have identifiable learning disabilities. Others find learning as easy as pie. What's the bottom line? Somewhere in their lives are unmet physical or emotional needs that take precedence over the drive to learn and the resulting joy of doing so.

When the roots of a tree lack sufficient water, nutrients, and safety, the branches will rarely yield fruit. The tree may survive, but that's about all.

As educators, we cannot raise children for their parents. We can't police communities to make them safe. We can't force overprotective parents to ground their helicopters and expect more from their children. We can't cure serious mental health problems or addictions. We don't have the resources to eliminate the serious economic woes facing so many families.

We can provide school and classroom environments where our students... at least during the time they are with us... get what they need. We can also provide some guidance and practical skills to the many parents who are highly motivated to help their children. The game plan below represents a limited number of high payoff strategies that enable us to stay sane while getting at the root issues.

PROVIDE EYE CONTACT, SMILES, AND FRIENDLY TOUCH

Are students more likely to take the risks required for learning when they feel emotionally connected with their teachers? Experiment with greeting students each and every day with the three elements of human bonding: brief eye contact, a smile, and a handshake, high-five, or some other form of friendly, nonthreatening touch.

Many school people have become fearful of connecting with students in this way. A healthy fear of being sued or being viewed as perverts has led many to shy away from bonding with students in this pure and appropriate way. While this fear may be wise, we must also remember the following:

- We are talking about handshakes or high-fives. Nothing else.
- These are offered but never forced upon the student.
- These are natural and public displays of enthusiasm and acceptance. Nothing is hidden or done privately.

Decades of research on human bonding has demonstrated that infants can actually die if they fail to receive healthy touch… even if every other need is met. While our students' physical lives may not depend on it, their emotional and educational lives do.

Apply the One-Sentence Intervention

At least twice a week, apply the one-sentence intervention as discussed in chapter three. That is, notice something unique about the student and share it with them. Whisper and use the format, "I noticed that you_____. I noticed that."

Sometimes this technique is confused with "catching them when they are good."

Providing rewards contingent on good performance remains the hallmark of many school and classroom behavior management programs. In fact, many schools require their teachers to provide "good behavior bucks" or other kudos when they see students do anything positive.

While this approach may be effective with some students in some situations, it often backfires with students having more significant, deep-seated problems, including academic apathy. When we praise or reward these students, they experience cognitive dissonance:

The teacher is really happy about what I did. But wait! If she's happy then I'm not in control. I can't let her think she's calling the shots. Besides… she's crazy thinking that I'm so great. If she just knew what a horrible kid I was… then she'd know better. I'll show her.

LOVE AND LOGIC EXPERIMENT:
I Believe In You

TEACHER: "I believe in you so much that I feel the need to nag."

STUDENT: (rolling eyes)

TEACHER: "Would it be okay if I occasionally nagged by whispering, 'How can I help'?"

Students who feel poorly about themselves and their relationships with others, experience massive anxiety when their performance is judged as good. The only way they can relieve this anxiety is by acting out in accordance with their preexisting negative self and world views.

Interestingly, high-achieving students also experience dissonance due to praise and rewards:

The teacher thinks I am so great. Oh… I better not risk falling off of this pedestal. I better take the safe route and not try anything too difficult. Being seen as smart and wonderful is way more important than learning new and challenging things.

The one-sentence intervention is all about noticing what the student values… not what we value. It's about demonstrating that we care for them as they are, rather than as we hope they will be. Have you noticed that people tend to find it safer to change when they're around others who love them and not just what they produce?

Call a Truce Over Learning

Have you ever known a student who had such strong, unresolved control needs that he was willing to fail an entire grade level of school just to prove to the adults in his life that he was the one in control? Have you ever met a student whose need for control is so great that she completed her assignments yet absolutely refused to hand them in? Have you ever known someone with such strong control needs that they believed you were trying to control them even when you weren't?

For learning to begin, the control battle must end. While reading the teacher-student dialogue below, consider how you might use your own words and your own style to convey this to a student. Remember that this is not about giving up on the student. It's about ending the battle so he or she will allow us to help.

TEACHER (with sincerity): "I need to apologize to you, Damien."

DAMIEN: "Why are you always on my case?"

TEACHER: "I think it's because I want you to do well and have forgotten who has to decide what type of life you end up living."

DAMIEN: "This is weird."

TEACHER (smiling): "Yeah. Who's the only one who can decide what type of life you have?"

DAMIEN: "Me."

TEACHER (still with sincerity): "Isn't that great? You get to decide. You call the shots. You get to decide what type of life you end up having."

DAMIEN: "I'll be fine."

TEACHER: "I hope so. You get to decide whether you learn the things that will give you more options in life... or don't learn them."

DAMIEN: "So."

TEACHER (with a caring smile): "I believe in you. I know that you can do well. I know you can give yourself more options in life. But... who needs to decide about that?"

DAMIEN: "Me."

TEACHER: "That's right. I'm going to stop fighting with you about your grades and stop trying to punish you into getting better ones."

DAMIEN: "It's about time."

TEACHER (still smiling): "I know. Would it be okay if I replaced all of that with just asking you if you need some help? Would it be okay if I came by your desk from time to time and asked, 'How can I help'?"

DAMIEN: "I guess… as long as you stay off my back."

TEACHER: "That sounds like a deal!"

DAMIEN: "And you'll give me 'A's?"

TEACHER: "I love your sense of humor, Damien. I assign students the grade they've earned… no higher or lower. The good news is that I like students the same regardless of how well or poorly they do in my class."

Stop Using Consequences or Punishment as an Achievement Motivator

When the horse dies, it's time to get off. Too frequently, people try to ride the broken-down mare called "consequences" or "punishment" in an attempt to motivate these students. If this actually worked, we'd be for it. Sadly, it creates more harm than good, including a classroom dynamic where students punish their teacher for punishing them. Have you ever seen a tough student "get even" with a teacher by causing constant low-level disruptions? Have you ever seen one "consequence" their teacher by luring her into unwinnable arguments or even shouting matches? We wonder how many office referrals start in the following way:

The student isn't working but isn't bothering others.

The teacher approaches the student and says something like, "You need to get to work."

The student doesn't comply.

The teacher issues a threat: "If you don't get to work…"

The student reacts with something like, "You can't tell me what to do."

The teacher reacts, "Don't talk to me like that!"

The student throws a fit and ends up in the office for discipline.

Does this need to happen?

> **LOVE AND LOGIC EXPERIMENT:**
> ## Soaking It Up
>
> STUDENT: (Is sitting in class refusing to work.)
>
> TEACHER (whispers): "I can see that you're learning in a different way today."
>
> STUDENT: "I ain't learning nothin'."
>
> TEACHER (smiling and continuing to whisper): "I'm such a great teacher that students can even learn when they aren't doing any work. The sad thing is that they have nothing to hand in for a grade. Just let me know how I can help."

No. Wise educators remember the solution to underachievement has far more to do with building relationships and meeting other underlying needs than using consequences or punishment. That's why they *don't* waste their time or energy trying to motivate these students with:

- Suspension from recess.
- In-school suspension or detention.
- Removal of other privileges.
- Expecting parents to provide consequences at home.
- Threats, lectures, or nasty looks.

When we aren't working so hard to keep track of implementing consequences… and dealing with the resulting ire from students and their parents… do we have a lot more time and energy left over for effective strategies?

Let's be clear: We are not suggesting students ever be immune from the logical and natural consequences of their actions.

When they act in ways that compromise the learning and safety of *others*, they must be held accountable. What we don't suggest is providing extra consequences or punishment when they are causing problems for *themselves* by failing to learn or complete assignments.

Use Sincere Empathy to Pass the Test

When we stop trying to control and coerce unmotivated students, it's quite likely their performance will become worse in the short term. How else can they test their new freedom? How else might they test your sincerity? How else will they learn to choose success over failure?

Some educators and parents balk at the thought of allowing kids to make mistakes. We believe the sooner they make them, the better. When is it best for a student to be given the freedom to see that their learning and their life is their own responsibility? Is it better if this happens after they leave home, or is it ideally best for this to happen in elementary school or even earlier? As we often say, "The price tag of mistakes goes up daily. It's far better for our children to learn when the consequences are small than when they are potentially life and death."

When we call a truce over learning, we end the control battle and simultaneously transition ownership of learning onto the student. Because this is a new responsibility, we can expect students to mess up. As we discussed in chapter four, our use of sincere empathy can dramatically increase the odds of success:

> *"Oh, Damien. I can't imagine how bad you must feel. I had to assign a zero because I never received your paper. Please let me know how I can help. I believe in you."*

Place Primary Emphasis on Successes and on Gifts

With reluctant or unmotivated students, what shapes learning most effectively? Is it focusing on success experiences or dwelling on failures? Is it concentrating on natural strengths or obsessing over weaknesses?

Teachers who understand the Love and Logic approach remember that the world's most successful people focus mostly on building upon their successes and honing their intuitive gifts. When it comes to their weaknesses and failures, these individuals learn from experience, but they spend no time beating their heads against the wall. A true Love and Logic teacher might share the following with his or her entire class:

> *"What's my biggest job as your teacher? Do you think it's to catch you when you do something wrong so you can correct it? Or do you think it's to catch you when you do something well and help you see how to do that even more often?*
>
> *"I'm the second type of teacher. I believe my biggest job is to help you discover what you do well so you can figure out how to turn that into a career someday.*
>
> *"That's why I walk around and point at things you've done. When I smile and don't say a thing, it means you did it right. Your job is to describe why you think you were successful.*
>
> *"Of course, sometimes I'll have to make you aware of something you did poorly or got wrong. Then I'll try to give you some helpful suggestions."*

Are people more willing to risk in their area of weakness if we've first built them up in their areas of strength? With our most resistant, apathetic students, educators are generally wise to notice at least ten success experiences for every one failure.

We also encourage educators to ask parents to focus on their child's successes and gifts. What might happen to the parent-child relationship, as well as the child's attitude toward learning, if a parent began the following plan?

> *"Son, I learned from your teacher that my biggest job right now is to help you identify what you do well. Each day I'd like you to pick just the parts of your schoolwork that you feel the best about... those parts that you got right. I think your teacher is correct. People can learn a lot by thinking about how they did things right.*
>
> *"What about the things you do poorly? Well... we're going to trust most of that stuff will get worked out by focusing on what you are doing well."*

It's important to note that this approach is not designed to be a way of providing praise or any type of tangible rewards. The adult simply describes what the child did correctly and asks, "How do you think you did that?" They refrain from unnatural, phony attempts to praise the child into succeeding more often. Here are some examples:

- "You completed number nine correctly. How did you do that?"
- "That sentence has a complete thought and a period at the end. How did you know to do that?"
- "You answered that Robert E. Lee was on the side of the Confederacy. How did you discover that?"
- "I can read the letter 'E' very clearly. How did you learn to do that?"

In essence, focusing on successes and strengths allows us to dramatically increase the odds of compliance when we say to a student, "I know this tends to be challenging for you. What are you good at? That's right! Even though this is harder for you, will you do this part of it just for me?"

Use Inquisitive "Conversations"

At the heart of most pervasive and chronic underachievement is anxiety... even downright fear. If each underachieving student carried a sign describing their experience on a daily basis, some would read, "I'm afraid of feeling stupid because I don't how to do this stuff." Others would say, "I'm afraid I won't do it perfectly." Many would say, "I'm so far behind that even trying to catch up is hopeless." Still others would indicate, "I'm afraid my peers will reject me if I succeed."

There are many effective strategies and assessment devices for determining student learning styles, aptitudes, and levels of achievement. Obviously these can play a major role in understanding how to best help students focus on their strengths while remediating skill deficits.

The assessment of academic anxiety or fear can be a bit trickier, and is often best achieved by having a series of brief inquisitive "conversations" with the student. The word "conversation" is used loosely here. Don't be dismayed if a student sits like a bump on a log, doing their best to act uninvolved or bored. The effectiveness of the "conversation" doesn't depend on their active participation. It depends on our sensitivity to their body language and demonstrating that we care and want to help. As you read, notice how the teacher makes it safe by talking about "some students."

TEACHER: "Thanks for visiting with me. I'd really like to help, and I was wondering if I could share some things I've noticed with other students in the past."

NOAH (sliding down in his chair): "I guess... fine."

TEACHER (with a caring, inquisitive tone): "I've noticed some students avoid doing their work because they don't understand how to do it and are embarrassed about that."

At this point the teacher allows silence, resisting the urge to ask, "Is that you?"

NOAH: "Not me."

TEACHER (with a caring smile): "I've just seen that with some other students. Other kids avoid doing their work because they don't like to do anything that they can't do perfectly."

The teacher allows more silence.

TEACHER (with sincere empathy): "Some students avoid doing their work because they are feeling so bad about other things going on in their life that they just can't bring themselves to try anything at school."

Again, the teacher allows a bit of awkward, yet powerful silence.

NOAH: "I just think school is pathetic."

TEACHER (with calmness and sincerity): "I'm glad you feel you can be honest with me, Noah. If you can think of any way I can help, please let me know."

NOAH (acting extremely unimpressed): "Yeah."

TEACHER: "Oh, by the way, who believes in you?"

NOAH (rolling his eyes): "You do."

A series of brief "conversations" such as this can go a long way toward building relationships and developing an intuitive sense of why the student is refusing to work. When this happens we can begin to experiment with possible solutions.

TEACHER: "Noah, I might be totally wrong about this. Can I share it anyway?"

NOAH: "Yeah… I guess."

TEACHER: "It seems like you start to bother other kids or put your head down on your desk when we do something

which requires you to write. I wonder if writing
might be challenging for you."

NOAH: "It's just stupid."

TEACHER (focusing on Noah's feelings): "I can see that you really
don't like it."

NOAH: "No… I hate it!"

TEACHER: "And what are you really good at?"

NOAH: "Skateboarding."

TEACHER: "I'd love to hear more about that. It would really help
me with my son. He always wants me to talk with
him about it, but I don't know anything about it.
Do you think we could trade?"

NOAH: "Huh?"

TEACHER: "Well, maybe you could teach me about skateboarding
so that I don't feel silly with my son and I could
teach you a bit about writing so school feels better
for you."

NOAH (doing his best not to smile): "Well, I guess. But I'm
really busy."

Remember the Ninety-Five Percent Rule

For reluctant students to become motivated to learn and achieve,
they must experience success at least ninety-five percent of the
time they apply a reasonable level of sustained effort. When
this doesn't occur, the brain's built-in reinforcement system never
has a chance to provide the wonderful feelings of achievement
many of us take for granted. Can you imagine going through
life on a day-to-day basis never experiencing the satisfaction of
seeing yourself perform a job well done? There's one word for
this feeling: Hopelessness.

Given the extreme time and energy demands placed on today's
educators, we almost feel ashamed suggesting they attempt to
tailor instruction to the needs of individual students. We are

also aware many of the mandated curricula are paced in such a way that doing so can be challenging. With this acknowledged, we also know that nobody continues to try when they never experience success.

Help them Develop the Perspiration Perspective

Some people live by what we call the "Las Vegas Plan." The idea here is that success and its perks largely depend on chance… on factors beyond their control. These folks wait around for a lucky break. Since they believe success is determined by the roll of the dice or by the hand someone else deals them, they consider hard work and perseverance irrelevant.

Other individuals live by the "Perspiration Plan." While they have a healthy sense that many things are beyond their immediate control, they do their best to make success happen through sweat. These highly motivated people believe success doesn't depend on the skills of their teachers, the niceness of their employers, the lucky breaks they receive… or even how smart they are. Instead, success is mostly determined by how hard they work, how much they persevere, and how many times they pick themselves up after blowing it.

Just a bit earlier in this chapter, we discussed the importance of focusing on successes and asking students, "How did you do that?" This focus gains its supreme power when we also offer three possible options for answering that question:

- "I worked hard."
- "I kept trying."
- "I've been practicing."

Each of these potential answers is the same. They all come down to perspiration being the cause of the student's success. Our goal is not to say one of these to the student, but to get *them* to utter the words.

Reaching Apathetic Students

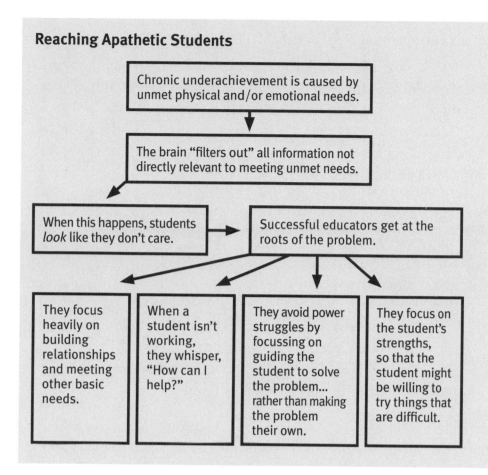

What we say is our reality. What students say will become theirs.

Consider the following example:

TEACHER: "Allie, you found the right answer to that word problem. How did you do that?"

ALLIE: "I don't know."

TEACHER (pointing at the bulletin board): "Which one? Did you work hard, keep trying, or have you been practicing?"

ALLIE: "Uh… I guess… I don't know."

TEACHER (smiling): "If you did know which one would it be?"

ALLIE: "Uh… I guess… Uh… I kept trying?"

TEACHER: "I bet that feels good."

STUDY THE BOOK *FROM BAD GRADES TO A GREAT LIFE!*

In this book, I (Charles) describe a variety of additional strategies for building intrinsic motivation. It's mostly a book for parents about why character is the foundation for success in school and life. It'll give you more ideas for the classroom and plenty of suggestions for parents who are seeking your help.

The bottom line

In a nutshell, success with unmotivated students comes down to a process:

> Build positive **relationships**…
> • so students will take the **risks** required to learn…
> • so they will have opportunities to **struggle**…
> • so they can experience the good feelings of **achievement**…
> • so they can see that hard work and perseverance lead to **great feelings of accomplishment.**

CHAPTER TEN

Success with Challenging Parents

While no one at Switzer Elementary was brave enough to admit it, most had tried to hide from Mrs. Hoshtel. There were rumors that Mr. Burrell, a sixth grade teacher, had ducked under his desk when he heard her coming. Perhaps it was no coincidence that Ms. Simons, the secretary, needed to use the office restroom… for nearly two hours… every time Mrs. Hoshtel's green SUV appeared in the student drop-off/pick-up lane (a.k.a. "helicopter landing pad").

Mrs. Hoshtel did not appear to be an old-fashioned helicopter parent. She presented like the latest jet-powered attack model, equipped with heat-seeking missiles and twin 50-caliber armor-piercing machine guns. She didn't simply rescue her little Liam… she annihilated anyone perceived as being potentially threatening to his fragile self-esteem.

It was Friday 4:47p.m., and Debi looked up just in time to witness Lynne bursting into her classroom. It was clear from the young teacher's face that all was not well with her world.

"I can't believe it! I just can't believe it!" Lynne perseverated. "I just got hit by a train."

Debi was alarmed. "What's going on? Are you okay?"

"Yeah... I guess... I mean... well... I can't believe what just happened with Liam's mom. I tried to explain to her what was going on, but she mowed me over. The conference was a disaster. She's so angry, blaming me for everything. I couldn't get anywhere with her. Every time I tried to explain the reasons for his bad grades and problems with other students, she interrupted me mid-sentence with some accusation. It was crazy."

"I know you really care about your kids, so I bet that hurts."

"Yeah..." Lynne replied, "and now she's even claiming I lose his assignments... that he's turning them in but I lose them... and I make him too nervous to do his work in class. That's why she thinks he's doing so poorly. It's crazy. I couldn't convince her otherwise."

"That sounds horrible."

"It was. She even told me that I have no business teaching and she's going to get me fired."

The Death of a Dream

Was Mrs. Hoshtel acting crazy because she was demented, ill, and mean spirited, or was she behaving this way because she was grieving the death of someone precious... the son of her dreams? While some parents act crazy because they are crazy, most who act crazy are sane and reasonable people, experiencing great pain as a result of their child's problems. No parent anticipates having a child who struggles with learning... or has serious behavior problems... or has difficulty relating to their peers... or has a mental or physical disability.

LOVE AND LOGIC EXPERIMENT:

When a Parent Asks, "Are You a Parent?"

Teachers who are not parents often feel intimidated when a parent asks in an accusatory tone, "Do you have kids?"

Experiment with smiling and responding, "No... but I was a challenging kid. It's a wonder that my parents survived all of those years."

As I (Jim) and Dr. Foster Cline were initially developing the Love and Logic approach, we witnessed the opening of a nearby school for young children with severe special needs. The administrator of the program soon admitted that over eighty percent of their time was being spent dealing with upset parents demanding additional special accommodations for their children. Every effort was made to satisfy these demands. But regardless of these efforts, there was no decrease in the number of upset parents or demands for additional accommodations.

A wise psychologist consulted with their team of teachers, and helped them discover the heart of the issue: Their school was the first place where these generally good and loving parents were forced to face the true severity of their children's difficulties. While the staff had always done their best to be professional and compassionate, they were being seen as the bearers of bad news. Dreams were being shattered. Parents were grieving.

The psychologist asked the staff to imagine the types of dreams parents usually have for their children. They answered... . Our dream for our children is that they...

- do well in school.
- are responsible.
- are healthy and happy.
- have friends.
- enjoy good self-esteem.
- do not have the problems we had as kids.
- are loving and cooperative.
- do well in sports.
- someday get good jobs.
- someday have their own kids and become good parents.

After this exercise, the teachers became more aware of the grief these parents were experiencing. They began to view these people in a different light. Rather than seeing them as pains, they began to see their pain.

Instead of seeing them as pains,
try to see their pain.

Back to Mrs. Hoshtel

"Lynne, are you interested in hearing something that really changed how I work with parents?" Debi asked.

"I'll take anything. I can't handle another conference like that!"

Debi described a Love and Logic conference and how I (Jim) had taught about what happened at the special needs preschool.

"But she was just so mean!" Lynne interrupted. "It's going to be difficult to shake the feeling of being bulldozed like that."

"It's not easy. You're right. We're human… but this does give us an amazing chance to help kids by building relationships with their parents."

"I guess that makes sense… but she kept denying that Liam plays any role in the problem. She got madder every time I tried to help her see it. Did I also tell you that she wants me to give him a blue algae tablet when he starts getting restless? I guess she heard it cures ADD."

Stages of Parental Grief and Loss

Most people act a bit crazy and irrational when grieving. This is part of the normal and healthy process of eventually arriving at a sense of acceptance over the loss. We as educators are well served to recognize the stages as we visit with parents.

DENIAL

"Not my child!"
"We never have these problems at home."
"What are the other kids in class doing? Did they start it?"

The pain of accepting the truth is often too unbearable to face... at least initially. Denial is a healthy coping mechanism... as long as it doesn't become the final destination. It allows us to face the pain of loss in a gradual and tolerable way, rather than being overwhelmed with emotions.

ANGER

"You don't care!"

"You never do anything to help my child!"

"You're racist!"

"You're hearing from our lawyer!"

Anger indicates the parent is making progress... that their denial is wearing off. We as educators can choose to take this anger personally or opt to remember it's simply part of the process.

BARGAINING

"If she just had another teacher, she'd be doing fine."

"If you just guide his hand over the paper when you want him to complete something, he can do it. Just keep your hand on his, and he will get unstuck. Have you tried that?"

"If he just had a full time aide..."

"If you can send me hourly emails..."

This is the "if-then" stage: "If you just did _____, then all of our problems would quickly go away. "

The "solutions" demanded by the parent almost always require great effort on the part of everyone except the child. These "solutions" also represent knee-jerk reactions that will never get to the root of the problem.

When teachers gracefully say "no" to implementing the parent's ideas... or when they inevitably fail to bring about a miraculous transformation in the child... the parent often revisits the anger stage. They project blame upon the teacher, rather than accepting the truth.

When a Parent has a Bad... But Not Horrible Idea

There are times when parents suggest "accommodations" that aren't horrible but are sure to be ineffective.

We all learn from making mistakes, experiencing the consequences, and feeling empathy from others around us. Parents are no different. Sometimes it's wise to suggest a time-limited "experimental period" where we agree to do exactly what the parent wants us to do... so that they can see firsthand that it isn't effective.

The key is to document your good faith efforts to implement the accommodation and demonstrated compassion when things don't go as hoped.

This doesn't necessarily mean we've done anything wrong, and it doesn't mean the parent is completely nuts or incorrigible. It simply indicates the grief process is moving along in a normal and predictable fashion.

DEPRESSION

"We've tried everything... and nothing works."

"We just don't know what to do."

While we feel for any parent who is this discouraged, we also know they are nearing acceptance and openness to our ideas.

ACCEPTANCE

"We love him so much... and we know he's not always so easy to love."

"You deserve a medal for how hard you've worked with her."

Acceptance is never arrived at without the pain that comes from visiting and revisiting denial, anger, bargaining, and depression. Parents typically arrive here faster when we avoid becoming defensive and listen with empathy.

How We View People Makes A Difference

Debi and Lynne met for coffee on Sunday morning. "I guess if I'm going to be a teacher in this day and age," Lynne sighed, "I better get good at dealing with difficult people."

Debi smiled. "Yeah, for some reason it always seems as if adults are harder to work with than the kids."

Lynne nodded. "I think you're right. I mean, we even have some staff that… well… and my boyfriend… well, let's not go there."

"I hear ya," Debi grinned, "but something you said left me concerned. It was about resigning yourself to having to work with difficult people. It seems like you're really burdened."

"Well… I'm not happy about it."

Debi countered with an important question: "Will you be less stressed and more effective if you view people like Liam's mom as hurting rather than as difficult?"

Lynne paused to think. "Do you really think it makes that much difference?"

"It did for me. When I stay in the habit of seeing through to the hurt inside, I don't take what they do so personally. I also find it a lot easier to stay empathetic and calm."

When we view people as hurting
rather than difficult, we are far more likely
to remain empathetic and calm.

"Yeah, I wouldn't choose to be that mom. It must be really difficult to be in her shoes every day."

Debi provided an experiment: "If you're interested, spend some time this evening imagining how challenging it must be for her. Then see if this helps you feel a bit less stressed about the situation. I know it's a hard experiment, but I think it might help. When I have some time, I can also share a process you might want to try with Mrs. Hoshtel. It might even turn her into your biggest supporter."

Lynne laughed. "Is that really coffee you're drinking? Now you're delusional."

A Win-Win Process

I (Jim) discovered early in marriage that I was tempted to use my mouth more than my ears. When I fell into this temptation, things never went well. When my wonderful wife, Shirley, was upset, it always made things worse when I tried to make sense. It took me far too many years to learn that she needed my empathy… not my expertise.

> *When people are upset, they need our empathy,*
> *not our expertise.*

Early in my teaching career, I also discovered I had the same unfortunate tendency when I found myself face to face with an upset parent. Almost automatically, I'd find myself exerting massive amounts of energy solving problems rather than listening. This worked with a few parents. Mostly it blew up in my face.

When I first became a school principal, I discovered something that made me feel a bit better for a very brief period of time. I noticed most of the teachers I was tasked with leading had the same problem. It wasn't just the guys. It was the women, too. I felt better about myself for a moment. I wasn't alone.

Then I had a horrible thought: *My life with the parents at my new school was going to get worse and worse if we all didn't learn some new skills!*

It was about this time that I became privy to the parent problems over at the special needs preschool. From this, I realized most of the "difficult" parents we were facing were dealing with grief and loss. The stages were so recognizable in their behavior

Never Make an Angry Parent Wait

- Wait for them outside of the front door of the school.
- Never have them cool their heels waiting for you in the office.
- Never have them sent down to your room by the secretary.
- Always be the first adult they see when they pull up to the school.
- Greet them with eye contact, a smile, and a handshake.
- Make them feel special.

that they could have been used as examples in a textbook for grief counselors. I began to see that we first needed to show how much we cared before we demonstrated how much we knew.

STEP ONE: LEAD WITH EMPATHY AND COLLECT INFORMATION.

Where there's no sincere empathy, there's no Love and Logic. Empathy soaks up emotions. It changes brain functioning, moving the lion's share of neurological activity from the limbic system (devoted to emotions and fight or flight) to the prefrontal cortex (devoted to attention, self-control, and complex reasoning). We possess the power to change another person's "mind"… that is as long as we replace "trying to reason" with "trying to understand."

Empathy soaks up emotions.

Highly effective educators identify one to three authentic empathetic responses for use with upset parents. Examples include:

- "I can't imagine how upsetting this must be."
- "I bet it's incredibly frustrating to hear that_____."
- "I'm hearing that you are very angry about this."

Leading with empathy opens the door for parents to feel free to express their emotions. That's why wise educators aren't shocked when they hear some things that sting. They aren't surprised when they hear illogical comments. They aren't shocked when they hear stuff that sounds crazy.

The key to success is to get the parent talking as much as possible. The more they talk and express their emotional point of view, the more likely they'll eventually calm to accept a more rational point of view.

The more the parent talks and expresses their emotions, the quicker they will become calm enough to consider solutions.

A helpful strategy involves readying ourselves with four phrases for use in response to just about anything a parent might say:

- "Tell me more."
- "Help me understand."
- "What would you like to see here?"
- "How long have you felt this way?"

Over the past three decades, we've known many educators who've taped these phrases to their desks. Some schools have them posted in the staff workroom. We often joke, if you're fortunate to have a large percentage of challenging parents at your school, you may want to have these tattooed along the inside of four fingers.

Let's imagine how these might be applied:

A parent accuses, "You never explain anything. How is he supposed to learn anything if you don't teach?"

Which of the following should you use?

a. "Tell me more."
b. "Help me understand."
c. "What would you like to see here?"
d. "How long have you felt this way?"
e. Any of the above.

The correct answer is "e." Just pick the first one that comes to mind.

Another example:

"He's really sensitive. He needs more praise. You need to tell him how great he is… give him some strokes… at least once every twenty minutes. That's what our therapist said."

Okay… after careful consideration, which response could be used? Again, it's "e": Any of the above.

It doesn't matter which one you use.

Most of us tend to freeze up when a parent says something confrontational or completely counter to common sense. When this happens, falling back on any one of these four phrases allows us to keep the ball rolling in a healthy direction. Just use the first one that comes to mind. Then remember…

- don't interrupt.
- don't try to defend yourself.
- don't try to reason with the parent.

It's also helpful to ask plenty of thoughtful questions:

- "How did this come to your attention?"
- "How did your child explain this to you?"
- "What was your initial reaction?"
- "Have there been other problems like this in the past?"
- "What kind of things have you tried so far?"
- "What is the best way that you see me helping with this?"
- "If you could have it your way, what would it look like?"

STEP TWO: SLOW THINGS DOWN.

As the parent is venting, it's often helpful to ask, "I want to make sure I am hearing you correctly. May I take some notes?"

Write exactly what the parent is saying… exactly. Don't paraphrase or summarize. Write it down verbatim.

Obviously this is difficult to do… and it takes time. That's precisely why it's so effective. Since we write so much slower than an angry person can speak, we slow the process and calm emotions by occasionally saying, "I'm sorry, I didn't get that. This is important. Will you repeat that so that I can get all of this down?"

STEP THREE: PROVE THAT YOU'VE LISTENED.

From time to time ask, "I want to make sure I'm getting this correct. Is it okay if I read it back to you?"

The parent needs to hear their exact words.

Start with, "Let's see if I've got this." End with, "Is there anything I've missed?"

> *"Let's see if I've got this right. You said, 'I'm not fair, I give other kids preferential treatment, I have no business teaching, and you are surprised I have a license, that I…' Is there anything I've missed?"*

Doing this (without any sarcastic voice inflection or defensive body language) allows us to prove we've listened. It also helps the parent reflect on how they are truly sounding. We've heard many parents reply, "Well… I didn't really mean that. What I really meant was…"

Typically, the parent's second version is less emotional and more rational than their first. Regardless, this allows us to always look back on the interaction and say to ourselves, "I was a class act."

No skill or technique will work with every person all of the time. This approach increases the odds for success but doesn't guarantee that the parent will see our point of view. Some people apply this and other techniques in an attempt to control others.

Wiser people do so primarily because they want to control themselves. They realize they can't ensure that all goes well, but their focus is to consistently treat others in dignified and respectful ways... regardless of how others react. Which person will suffer more frustration? Which will struggle with chronic feelings of failure?

In its deepest and most accurate sense, Love and Logic has nothing to do with changing or controlling other people. It's all about living life in a way where we can consistently say to ourselves, "I was a class act."

> *Love and Logic is about handling situations so well*
> *that we can consistently look in the mirror and say,*
> *"I was a class act."*

Frequently, Love and Logic techniques allow us to reflect on situations with, "I was a class act, and things turned out well."

Other times... because we are working with complex situations and unpredictable human beings... we end up reflecting, "I was a class act... and things still went miserably... but I was a class act!"

STEP FOUR: CHECK FOR ENTRY INTO THE THINKING STATE.

The previous steps in the process provide an opportunity for parents to be heard and to feel respected. As such, they are designed to gently move parents from the "emotional state" (the limbic system) to the "thinking state" (the prefrontal cortex).

But how do we know this neurological shift has taken place? Ask, "Would you like my thoughts?"

If the parent has begun to move into the thinking state, he or she will say something like, "Yes," or "I guess so." If so, it's time for step five.

If you sense even a slightest iota of resistance, ask, "It seems as if there may be something else you'd like to share. Is that the case?"

If necessary, return to step one.

STEP FIVE: BEGIN PROBLEM SOLVING.

Parents who sense the teacher or the school is willing to view their child's problems as unique, tend to be much more supportive and cooperative. Open this step by suggesting that there are usually many solutions to a given problem, depending on the child. It's possible that looking at different solutions will trigger more emotions on the parent's part. If that's the case, go back to step one and do a good job of listening to bring the parent back into the problem-solving discussion.

One of the most challenging parts of working with upset or resistant people is resisting the urge to move too quickly toward this final step. As my teachers and I (Jim) began to embrace and refine this process, we discovered something: Most of the time the real problem was not what we thought it was when the conversation started. The most common reason problem solving fails is the problem was never accurately identified. When we rush and fail to listen effectively, massive amounts of time, energy, and other resources are wasted attempting to solve the wrong problem.

> *The most common reason problem solving fails is that the actual problem was never accurately identified.*

We also discovered the real problem usually had far more to do with the parent's fear, insecurity, grief, or pain than the specifics of what we were doing with their child.

After taking time to reflect on her coffee conversation with her mentor, Debi, Lynne began to soften a bit toward Mrs. Hoshtel, Liam's mom. She probably is hurting a lot, she admitted to herself.

Equipped with the process discussed above, she even called Mrs. Hoshtel to schedule a face-to-face meeting. As she prepared, she reminded herself of a key truth related to all relationships:

Success is not determined by how others react.
Success is determined by how maturely I do.

While it's true that we cannot make other people behave, this win-win process does have an amazing track record of taming parents who appear to be hostile helicopters or demanding drill sergeants. A high school teacher commented:

"I can't believe how many parents come in as tigers, growling and going for blood, and end up crying on my shoulder. Many have said, 'This is the first time anybody at any of his schools actually listened.' There's nothing more gratifying than seeing the relief on a parent's face when they begin to believe that you really care."

Preventing Problems Before They Happen

We chose to write this chapter backwards: We started with responding to parents after they're already upset. Since none of us have time to provide extensive grief counseling or psychotherapy while also trying to perform all of our other job duties, it makes practical sense that most of our efforts ought to go toward fire prevention.

Calming Upset Parents

Step One: Lead with empathy and collect information.

Listen and show that you care.

Step Two: Slow things down.

Take notes and write exactly what the parent is saying... verbatim.

Step Three: Prove that you've listened.

Ask, "I want to make sure that I'm getting this correct. Is it okay if I read it back to you?"

Step Four: Check for entry into the thinking state.

Ask, "Would you like my thoughts?"

Step Five: Begin problem solving.

Don't be surprised if you need to revisit the previous steps.

BUILD RELATIONSHIPS BEFORE PROBLEMS DEVELOP

It's always best to begin connecting before problems arise. If you serve a relatively small number of students, you may have the luxury of doing the following with each and every parent:

- Call during the first week of school and describe something unique you've noticed about their child. In other words, use the one-sentence intervention with the parent: "I noticed that Liam really enjoys drawing. I noticed that."

- Continue to make these voice-to-voice or face-to-face contacts as frequently as possible. Do this most often with the parents of your more challenging students. Also share some positive things you've noticed about their child's behavior. "Yesterday Liam held the door open for other students as they were coming back from recess." Specific and detailed descriptions like this are always more credible than vague ones like, "Liam is polite" or "Liam is courteous."

- While there is nothing inherently wrong with making these contacts via email or notes home with the student, remember that voice-to-voice… and particularly face-to-face contacts… are always far more powerful.

- Use the one-sentence intervention with all of your students. The more they love you, the more likely they'll share their love for you with their parents.

How does a teacher accomplish this when they serve a large number of students?

They prioritize.

During the first week of school… or better yet before… note the students who seem most likely to display behavioral or achievement-related problems. Trusting your gut-level intuition, rank these students in terms of the level of difficulty they will likely present. This list is strictly confidential, meant for your eyes only. Once you've identified your highest need students, target them and their parents with heavy doses of sincere relationship building.

AVOID NOTIFYING PARENTS ABOUT PROBLEMS VIA TEXTS OR EMAILS

Texts and emails are the kiss of death when it comes to describing a child's problem to their parent. They are wonderful for scheduling appointments, or perhaps sharing positives from time to time, but they're often misinterpreted when used to communicate "issues." Effective problem solving over deeply emotional issues always requires face-to-face interaction. It's impossible to move a parent from the emotional state to the thinking state without connecting in this more personal and compassionate way. They need to truly see… truly experience… how much you care.

COMMUNICATE HOW YOU OPERATE BEFORE YOUR STUDENTS DO

Too frequently, students go home and provide less-than-accurate descriptions of how we run our classrooms. Unlike years ago, these days many parents believe their children rather than doing some fact checking. Once beliefs get planted, they tend to grow regardless of the facts. This is why we strongly encourage teachers to start the year by equipping all of their parents with a letter that reads something like the following:

Dear Mrs. Hoshtel,

I'm so thankful to have Liam in my class this year. Before too much time goes by, I want you to know a bit about how I run my classroom. First of all, students are valued for their unique gifts, and I do my best to run my classroom according to the Love and Logic approach. When you visit, you will see this poster on the wall:

HOW I RUN MY LOVE AND LOGIC CLASSROOM

- I will treat you with respect so that you will know how to treat me.
- Feel free to do anything that doesn't cause a problem for anyone else (in the known universe).
- If you cause a problem, I will ask you to solve it.
- If you can't solve the problem or choose not to, I will do something.
- What I do will depend on the special person and the special situation.
- If you feel something is unfair, whisper to me, "I'm not sure that's fair," and we will talk.

I'm always willing to visit with a student about something they view as unfair. Depending on the merits of their case, I may or may not change my course of action.

Students learn and grow only when they experience some manageable struggles. Instead of trying to ensure that your child never experiences disappointments, frustrations, or other difficulties, I will do my best to help them learn to cope with these challenges by solving problems. When kids overcome the struggles they face, they develop confidence and healthy self-esteem.

Please know that I take no joy in seeing students struggle with challenges. I simply know they need them in order to learn how to become happy, strong, and confident. You have my guarantee that I will treat your child with empathy and with great dignity.

Sincerely,

DON'T EXPECT PARENTS TO SOLVE SCHOOL PROBLEMS AT HOME

Too frequently, educators provide overwhelmed... and often less-than-skilled... parents with homework they cannot complete. This "homework" often sounds like:

- "He had a horrible day, and we really need you to follow up with consequences at home."
- "You need to make sure he's completing his homework."
- "We need you to talk with him about the importance of being more cooperative at school."
- "He's had a bad attitude, and it's important you address this."

If you want enemies, this is the best way to make it happen. Consider the following alternative:

TEACHER: "Ms. Wilkins, I'm so thankful you've taken the time to visit with me face to face about Josiah. Do you feel like I've listened to you?"

PARENT: "Yes. I appreciate it. I'm just so frustrated with him."

TEACHER: "Parenting is so challenging. I can see how much you love him. Would you like some thoughts?"

PARENT: "Sure, but I just don't know what is going to help."

TEACHER: "I don't want this to be more of a problem for you, so I have some ideas about what we can do here at school to help."

(The teacher describes what he/she will do to help Josiah at school and listens as parent responds.)

TEACHER: "By the way… when you have a hard day at work does it help if you get consequences for it once you get home?"

PARENT: "Well… of course not! That would be crazy."

TEACHER: "I agree. That's why we believe that what happens at school is usually best handled at school. Then parents and their kids can spend more time loving and enjoying each other, rather than stressing over what happened someplace else."

PARENT: "But what do I do at home?"

TEACHER: "If you want some ideas for making your life easier with Josiah at home, we have some Love and Logic resources that can really help. Just let me know if you want to borrow any from our resource library. The nice side effect is that they often help kids to be more successful at school."

What's another sad result of expecting parents to handle problems that take place at school? Students begin to believe their teachers aren't strong enough... or don't care enough about them... to truly handle their misbehavior.

ENCOURAGE PARENTS TO RECEIVE OUR FREE *INSIDER'S CLUB* TIPS

As a school principal, I (Jim) quickly discovered that parents were usually more cooperative with our mission when they truly understood what it was. I also found many were appreciative when I offered some strategies for reducing their parenting stress at home. As a result, I began to author a weekly parenting tip in our school newsletter *(Principally Speaking)*.

Parents who read these tips were less likely to march into my office, demanding to know why we were running a concentration camp. They began to see that we were committed to empathy and helping kids learn to feel good about themselves by overcoming struggles. Of course, there was a small number who truly hated my tips... and they were vocal. This worked out well, too, as we weren't caught off guard when they had their fits.

I wrote the original *Principally Speaking* tips in the early 1980s. We've written thousands of new and unique ones on a variety of topics since that time. Approximately ten years ago, we began to offer them via weekly emails to anyone who signs up for our *Insider's Club*. They are free, and they're a wonderful way to gain more cooperation at your school.

PROVIDE LOVE AND LOGIC PARENTING CLASSES

The more successful parents are with their children, the smoother and more effective your school will be. Our parent-training curriculum offers a step-by-step approach to providing parent training that anyone can facilitate. Parents like it because it's simple, practical, and full of entertaining videos. They can giggle and learn at the same time.

A longtime Love and Logic teacher, Mrs. Garcia, provided an example of how this program impacted one of their more challenging parents:

> **LOVE AND LOGIC EXPERIMENT: "How Long Have You Been Teaching?"**
>
> Newer teachers often feel intimidated when a parent asks sarcastically, "How long have you been teaching?"
>
> Experiment with smiling confidently and saying, "I've been teaching for ____ and I use an approach that's based on research and over one hundred years of combined experience. It's called Love and Logic. It's all about dignity and respect."

"Our principal just doesn't believe in suspending kids, but Ty pushed him to the limit. This kid was small even for a second grader. That's why we were amazed he'd managed to jump hard enough on one of the urinals in the boys' bathroom to knock it off the wall. It may have been a bit loose to start with, but he must have worked extremely hard to break it off. Of course, water went everywhere, and Ty went home.

"Vandalism of this nature is a legal issue, so the authorities were called. We all braced ourselves for how Dad was going to react in the meeting.

"Our first surprise was that Dad brought Ty to the meeting. As the officer described the potential charges, and our principal outlined the cost of repairs, Dad didn't say a word. That was surprising, too. I figured he was giving deep thought to how he was going to blame us for the problem. I was wrong.

Instead, he turned to Ty and said, 'It looks like you have a really sad problem on your hands. How are you going to pay for all of this?'

"Ty was outraged, and replied, 'Well… it wasn't my fault… uh… it just fell off… uh, I don't know… and this is all stupid!'

"Dad replied, 'We're leaving, Ty. You've got a lot of work to do… and I love you too much to argue.'

"Apparently Ty spent most of that year doing a variety of less-than-pleasant jobs to reimburse his father for the cost of the damage."

What's the moral of this story? Never lose hope!

Theoretical Underpinnings and Evidence Base for Love and Logic

For more than five decades, severe disruptive behavior among youth has evolved from a relatively minor concern to a significant daily reality experienced by many (American Educator, 1996; Browne, 2013; Elam, Rose & Gallup, 1996; Lewis, Sugai, & Colvin, 1998; Walker, Colvin & Ramsey, 1995; Walker, Ramsey & Gresham, 2004). The National Institute of Mental Health (2002) and others (see Costello et al. 2001; Egger and Angold, 2006; U.S. Public Health Service, 2000), estimate that as many as 20% of American youth experience emotional and/or behavior problems. It's also estimated that approximately one in ten U.S. youth display some degree of more severe conduct problems (McMahon & Estes, 1997).

Considering these statistics, it's clear that many educators and parents are struggling with high levels of stress and lack of certainty regarding how to support children in the development of emotional and behavioral health (Graf et al, 2014; Shapiro, et al, 2008). Supporting these concerns is the growing frequency and intensity of emotional and behavioral problems observed by classroom educators (Bromfield, 2006; Cotton, 1990; Daniels,

2009; Fideler & Haselkorn, 1999; Fields, 2000; Garret, 2014; Lundeen, 2002).

In 1974, Foster Cline, M.D., a child psychiatrist treating severely disturbed children, and Jim Fay, a classroom educator and successful administrator sought to integrate diverse theoretical perspectives with the goal of developing a set of practical and effective strategies for helping parents support the emotional and behavioral health of their children. Their research-based approach was first formalized in the books *Parenting with Love and Logic* (Cline & Fay, 1990), *Parenting Teens with Love and Logic* (Cline & Fay, 1992), and *Teaching with Love and Logic* (Fay & Funk, 1995). Since that time, national and international demand for information on their approach has resulted in over fifty publications outlining its application to community parent-training initiatives and the improvement of academic achievement, parent-teacher relationships, classroom management, schoolwide culture, and marriage relationships. Currently, over 12,000 trainers offer this approach in the U.S, England, Mexico, Canada, Argentina, Brazil, Norway, Israel, Australia, and other countries.

Literature Review

The Love and Logic approach is based on the following process, integrating a wide array of established theory and research:

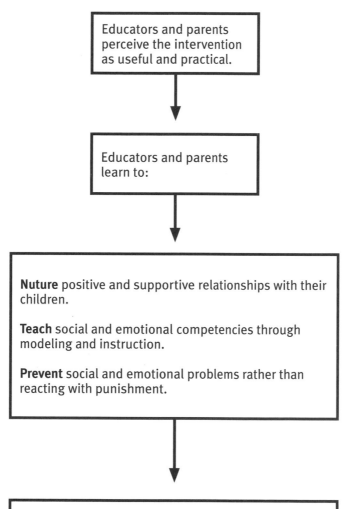

Educators and parents perceive the intervention as useful and practical.

Educators and parents learn to:

Nuture positive and supportive relationships with their children.

Teach social and emotional competencies through modeling and instruction.

Prevent social and emotional problems rather than reacting with punishment.

Children develop emotional and behavioral health/resiliency.

EDUCATORS AND PARENTS PERCEIVE
THE INTERVENTION AS USEFUL AND PRACTICAL.

Unfortunately, evidence-based approaches to parenting and classroom management are not always received with enthusiasm by those they are intended to help: parents and teachers. A common complaint is that these approaches take too much time and are impractical given the daily realities of homes and classrooms (Carnine, 1997; Kern & Manz, 2004).

The construct of social validity, according to Wolf (1978), defines the perceived value consumers place on a product. Interventions enjoying high social validity are not only perceived as being effective in experimentally controlled settings, but are also viewed as needed and applicable within the serious time limitations experienced by today's parents and educators (Albin et al., 1996; Graf et al, 2014; Kazdin et al, 1997; Schwartz & Baer, 1991; Spoth & Redmond, 1995; Witt & Elliott, 1985).

The international popularity of the Love and Logic approach suggests its social validity. Further, Clarke (2004), evaluating pre- and post-rating of parents trained in the approach observed that 91.4% of the 637 parents sampled reported imported improvements in their parental experience as a result of using the techniques learned in the course, and 76.5% reported improvements in their children's behavior. Anecdotes collected after the training also supported its perceived value:

> *I don't fly off the handle when dealing with him (son). I feel better instead of yelling all of the time. (p.1)*

> *I sent my paperwork home to my mother, who is keeping my children while I am in prison. She is now using Love and Logic. She enjoys the techniques with the children. She also stated that it helps a whole lot. (p.1)*

Offering Love and Logic training to 22 high school teachers, Johnson (2014) observed the following:

There was a statistically significant change between pre- and post-study responses (p=.0004) regarding teachers' perception of Love and Logic's importance to the school, starting with 75% unsure of its importance but ending with 65% indicating that it was important or very important. Similarly, 85% of the participants were undecided about their feelings concerning Love and Logic prior to the study, but 90% felt positive or very positive about it after the study (p<.0001.). (pp. 67-70)

Fay (2012) in a study of 2,409 parents representing a wide range of socio-economic and ethnic groups observed an 18% reduction in self-reported parenting stress (p<.001) and a 21% reduction in perceived child behavioral problems (p<.001) from pre-Love and Logic training to post. Statistically significant improvements (all p<.001) were also observed for the ratings listed below:

	Mean Ratings	
	Pre Love and Logic	Post Love and Logic
I find myself staying calm when I have to discipline.	2.89	3.62
I find myself feeling really stressed out.	3.09	2.41
My child argues and talks back.	3.44	2.63
My child throws tantrums or "fits."	2.95	2.30
My child completes chores without reminders or pay.	2.38	2.85

Participants also provided qualitative responses to, "Identify the most valuable thing you learned in this class." Select responses are included below:

- Remembering to whisper when I feel like yelling.
- Parenting is fun... not simply something to be endured.
- It's so much easier to not get into power struggles and arguments now that I know the way to do it. I feel a lot more calm about discipline.
- This class has helped me calm down and not get so frustrated!
- How to control myself, not my child. I react differently now and so does he. More positive interaction over conflict.
- Empathy, empathy, empathy! Because anger is my old pattern and because empathy helps *me* calmly think about appropriate actions/consequences.
- I loved it. I plan to bring my mother to a session. (p. 9)

EDUCATORS AND PARENTS LEARN TO NURTURE POSITIVE AND SUPPORTIVE PARENT-CHILD RELATIONSHIPS.

Positive adult-child relationships are the single most powerful environmental factor affecting the lifelong adjustment of children (Foshee & Bauman, 1994; Regalado and Halfon, 2002; Seeley, Stice, & Rohde, 2009; Sheeber, Hops, Alpert, Davis, & Andrews, 1997; Stice, Ragan, & Randall, 2004). In their recent study of 692 children in grades 3, 6, and 9, Hazel, et al (2014) observed that those experiencing positive and supportive parent-child relationships were far less likely to succumb to stress-related mental illness and behavior problems when confronted with common developmental stressors.

The adult-child relationship has also been observed as a powerful factor reducing the likelihood of academic failure (Clark, Dogan & Akbar, 2003; Heaven & Newbury, 2004; Robertson & Reynolds,

2010), drug use and other forms of delinquency (Huebner & Betts, 2002; Laundra, Kiger & Bahr, 2002), sexual risk-taking (Huebner & Howell, 2003; Ream & Savin-Williams, 2005; Karofsky, Zeng & Kosorok, 2000) and even internet and video game addiction (Kwon, Chung & Lee, 2009; Lee, Honk & Park, 2005).

Evidence strongly suggests that healthy relationships are most effectively fostered when educators and parents employ a dynamic balance between providing affection and necessary limits (Dishion 1990; Eisenberg and Murphy, 1995; Grusec & Goodnow, 1994; Maccoby & Martin, 1983; Richaud, Mesurado & Lemos, 2013). These findings support Baumrind's (1991; 1996) observation that effective parents employ an authoritative style rather than an authoritarian or permissive one. Cline and Fay (1990), two founding members of the Love and Logic process, encourage parents to adopt a "consultant" style of parenting, closely resembling Baumrind's authoritative style:

> *Love and Logic parents (and teachers) avoid the helicopter and drill sergeant mentalities by using a consultant style of parenting as early as possible in the child's life. They ask their children questions and offer choices. Instead of telling their children what to do, they put the burden of decision making on their kids' shoulders. They establish options within limits. Thus, by the time the children become teens, they are used to making good decisions. (p. 27)*

> *We as parents (and educators) must show our empathy... our sincere loving concern... when the consequences hit. That's what drives the lesson home with our children without making them feel as though we're not "on their side." (p.103)*

EDUCATORS AND PARENTS LEARN TO
TEACH SOCIAL AND EMOTIONAL COMPETENCIES.

Children are not born with the social and emotional skills required for success in life. When young people are explicitly shown these skills, are given opportunities to practice, and receive supportive feedback, dramatic improvements are often demonstrated in a variety of areas, including social skills (Gresham, Bao, & Cook, 2006) and anger management (Barnoski, 2004; Glick, & Gibbs, 2011; Mitchell, 2009).

More specifically, children must be given opportunities to observe and practice problem-solving skills. These opportunities require that (1) caring adults teach these competencies through modeling, instruction, and coaching; and (2) children are allowed to solve the problems they create (Foster, Prinz, & O'Leary, 1983; Kerr & Bowen, 1988) and children enjoy opportunities to develop self-efficacy (Bandura, 1977).

Spivak and Sure (1974) in their pioneering research on social problem solving, have noted that modeling and direct instruction are key strategies for teaching problem-solving skills. Similar propositions have been made by Bandura, 1976; Bandura & Jeffery, 1973; Cormier & Cormier ,1991. Therefore, the Love and Logic approach gives parents specific guidelines for using modeling, direct instruction, and feedback to teach the following problem-solving process:

1. Identify and define the problem.
2. Brainstorm solutions.
3. Evaluate each solution.
4. Implement the solution chosen.

Research supporting this problem-solving model is supported by D'Zurilla (1986), as well as Cormier and Cormier (1991).

EDUCATORS AND PARENTS LEARN TO
PREVENT SOCIAL AND EMOTIONAL PROBLEMS.

Highly effective approaches focus primarily on prevention, while less effective ones focus on punishment (Clunies-Ross et al, 2008; Lewis, Sugai & Colvin, 1998; Mayer & Sulzer-Azaroff, 1991). Interventions targeting the development of positive, supportive, and structured home environments provide powerful and cost-effective opportunities to prevent many of the social, emotional, behavioral, and academic problems facing our youth (Englund, Luckner, Whaley, & Egeland, 2004; Fan & Chen, 2001; Ganzach, 2000; Patterson, Reid, & Dishion, 1992; Pomerantz, Ng, & Wang, 2006; Walker, Colvin, & Ramsey. 1995; Walker, 1998.)

Schroeder and Kelley (2009) note:

An accumulating body of literature has shown that positive school discipline and parenting characterized by warmth, sensitivity, expressiveness, and adequate limit setting is associated with children's inhibition and ability to maintain attention (Eisenberg et al. 2005), self-control (Le Cuyer-Maus and Houck 2002), and behavior problems (Bradley and Corwyn 2005). (p.228)

Schroeder and Kelly's (2009) data corroborates these findings, showing significant and positive relationships between parental warmth, limits, and structure and the development of metacognitive skills essential for self-control. Clearly, many emotional and behavioral problems can be successfully managed, or prevented altogether, when parents (and educators) provide supportive relationships, caring climates, clear boundaries, supervision, appropriate consequences for violating boundaries, high yet developmentally appropriate expectations, and other resiliency factors (Barber & Olson, 1997; Benson et al, 1994; Benson, 2006; Larson, et al, 2004).

Cerdorian (2006), in her study of 374 parents, observed that those completing Love and Logic parenting classes reported dramatic and statistically significant reductions in parenting stress and behavior problems from pre-test to post.

Overall, stress related to the parenting role significantly decreased for parents in both treatment groups. While overall, the stress level of the comparison group increased over the time of the study, the parents who attended classes were less stressed in their parenting role by the completion of classes. Among treatment group parents of children one month to eleven years, 44.9%, and treatment group parents of youth 11 to 18, 43.5%, had clinically significant stress levels prior to the intervention of parenting classes. This decreased to 23.9% and 27.8% respectively, after the set of classes was completed. The study also supported a statistically significant decrease in perceived problem behavior for parents of children one month to eleven years. (pp. 105-106)

EDUCATORS AND PARENTS LEARN HOW TO ESTABLISH AND REINFORCE APPROPRIATELY HIGH EXPECTATIONS.

High expectations are essential to the prevention of emotional, behavioral, and academic problems in both home and school environments. While Rosenthal and Jacobson's (1968) classic Pygmalion study has been questioned on methodological grounds, the overall body of research conducted since that time clearly shows that the cultures of highly successful schools and homes are epitomized by high expectations (Bond & Saunders, 1999; Eccles, Wigfield, & Schiefele, 1998; Englund, Luckner, Whaley, & Egeland, 2004; Fan & Chen, 2001; Flouril, & Hawkes, 2008; Ganzach, 2000; Goyette & Xie, 1999; Good, & Nichols, 2001; Juang & Silbereisen, 2002; Mistry, 2007;

Sandefur, Meier, & Campbell, 2006; Zhang, Haddad, Torres, & Chuansheng, 2011). Notably, Doren, Gau, and Lindstrom (2012) followed a nationally representative sample of over eleven thousand 13- to 17-year-old special education students and their parents. Those whose parents communicated high expectations were at least twice as likely to graduate from high school, obtain a job, and engage in post-secondary education.

EDUCATORS AND PARENTS "SPEAK THE SAME LANGUAGE."

The challenges facing children are complex and multidimensional, affected by a variety of interacting systems. As such, intervention programs are far more likely to achieve effective and sustainable outcomes when they take a social-ecological perspective (Bronfenbrenner, 1979; Bronfenbrenner & Morris, 2006; Minuchin, 1985; Salzinger, Feldman, Stockhammer, & Hood, 2001) where protective factors are promoted in both the family and the school systems.

Crowe (2013), in a longitudinal study of 1,364 children in ten U.S. communities, observed that home-school cooperation in children's education, particularly when this cooperation begins early in the child's school career, contributes to significantly improved school success. The Love and Logic approach places heavy emphasis on the development of cooperative and consistent home and school environments where parents and educators are "speaking the same language" and working toward the same goal of fostering emotional and behavioral health among children and teens.

Training elementary school teachers, Weir (1997) observed high levels of teacher "buy-in" and use of the program in this school. After implementing this program: (a) 87% of teachers reported having more effective tools for managing student behavior; (b) 84% reported improved relationships with their students; (c) 68% reported decreased time spent managing behavior disruptions; (d) 71% reported increased time spent teaching curriculum; and (e) 82% reported having more control over discipline. Weir also observed a 48% decrease in the number of main office referrals for discipline during the first year this school applied the Love and Logic program.

Ridgeview Global Academy is a charter elementary school in Central Florida with over 600 students, grades K–5. During the 2001-2002 school year, staff were trained in the Love and Logic approach (Frier, 2003). After making this one change, dramatic improvement was observed: Referrals to the office for misbehavior decreased from 380 during the 2000–2001 school year to 116 during the 2002-2003 school year. A large reduction in referrals related to misbehavior on the school buses was also noted: 509 (2000-2001 school year) reduced to 142 (2002-2003 school year).

Spencer (2008), in a pilot study of thirty-three schools in Georgia, provided Love and Logic teacher training across elementary, middle, and high school levels:

75% of those trained agreed that Love and Logic "Positively impacts my school's learning environment."

71% agreed that the program "Positively impacts student achievement in my school."

75% agreed that "Instructional time is maximized throughout my school."

Using single-subject methodology, Mckenna (1997) examined the effects of a Love and Logic on a nine-year-old student's academic motivation, personal hygiene, classroom behavior, general demeanor, and self-concept. Teacher ratings and anecdotal observations revealed improved personal hygiene, an elevated frequency of positive peer and adult interactions and increased rates of homework completion. Pre- and post-test scores on the

Pierrs-Harris Self-Concept scale revealed a statistically significant 16-point improvement over the course of intervention.

Fay (2007) examined the results of training nearly 1,000 elementary and middle school teachers in the Love and Logic approach. Pre-test to post-ratings revealed statistically significant (all $p<.001$) for the ratings listed below:

	Mean Ratings	
	Pre Love and Logic	Post Love and Logic
The most behaviorally challenging students:		
argue with me.	3.18	2.74
interrupt me.	3.78	3.00
cooperate with me.	2.92	3.37
refuse to do their work.	3.04	2.59
solve their own problems with guidance.	2.80	3.43
As an educator, I find myself:		
being really stressed out and exhausted.	2.85	2.42
feeling confident that I can handle discipline problems.	3.62	4.09
enjoying good relationships with challenging students.	3.59	3.99

Recently, Johnson (2014) trained twenty-two high school teachers in the Love and Logic approach. Each was asked to provide ratings pre-training and post. Results of quantitative analyses revealed the following:

	t	p
I have a successful process to help disruptive students recover so they can get back on task.	6.64	<.0001
I enjoy students, even behaviorally challenging ones.	4.23	.0003
I am skilled with preventative interventions for a variety of student misbehaviors.	5.74	<.0001
I feel stressed because of problems with students.	-2.30	.0314
I am successful with students who get argumentative.	6.14	<.0001

Qualitative data also provided some promising results:

Many indicated that the technique worked in their classroom and beyond by stating they had "learned a better way to speak to students and others," that it deescalated defensiveness and rebellion in students and others, and it "had a positive impact on classes of students at school and at church." Many pointed out that it had a positive effect on their most challenging students, those they generally struggled to reach. For example, one participant commented, "I learned that I can't force anyone to do anything, so I have to reword my statements so I can actually enforce them." (p. 83)

Theoretical Roots of the Love and Logic Approach

The Love and Logic Theory is the result of over four decades of clinical practice and research integrating five theoretical perspectives:

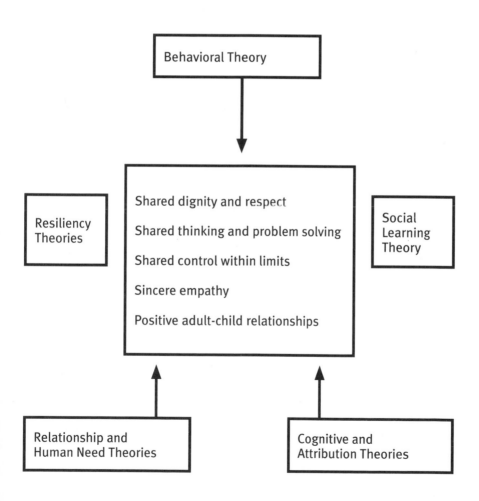

BEHAVIORAL THEORIES.

Antecedent and other contextual stimuli develop the ability to cue emotional and behavioral processes through the dynamic interplay between classical and operant conditioning (Pavlov, 1927; Skinner, 1953, 1974; Thorndike, 1911), and Watson & Rayner, 1920). As such, Fay and Cline argue that effective home and school interventions must address the role played by adults in these conditioning processes. Some primary objectives of the Love and Logic approach are as follows:

- Parents and teachers are paired with positive emotions and outcomes, so they automatically elicit these responses in the children they care for.
- Academic learning and responsible behavior are also paired with positive emotions and outcomes, so books and good behavior automatically elicit these emotions.
- Youth learn through wise application of reinforcement principles that good behavior is far more rewarding than bad.
- Once desired behaviors are established, maintenance and generalization is enhanced through the use of variable reinforcement schedules (Ferster & Skinner, 1957) and social reinforcement (Hall, Lund, & Jackson, 1968).

While behavioral theories and associated practices provide powerful strategies for establishing and maintaining desired behaviors, Fay and Cline were concerned with their inability to adequately address the roles played by vicarious learning and underlying cognitive and emotional processes. Therefore, they sought to address these potential shortcomings by integrating additional theory and research.

SOCIAL LEARNING THEORY.

In their classic study, Bandura, Ross, and Ross (1961) observed that children watching vignettes of an actor hitting a "Bobo" doll were more likely to exhibit aggressive behavior themselves. In later investigations, Bandura also documented that modeling results in far more than simple mimicry; children learn complex rules governing cause and effect by simply observing those around them (Bandura & Jeffery, 1973; Bandura, 1977). Based on these observations, Fay and Cline propose the following:

- What we do is at least as important as what we say.
- Therefore, parents and educators with a high skill level in Love and Logic place a heavy emphasis on controlling their own behavior so they can remain effective models.
- Effective parents and educators also engage in healthy self-care, including the appropriate setting and enforcement of boundaries, so they can remain positive models.

COGNITIVE AND ATTRIBUTION THEORIES.

Social Learning Theory provides a bridge from traditional behavioral theory to approaches recognizing the role played by cognitive processes. Of great interest is the construct of vicarious reinforcement, where the likelihood of an observed behavior being copied is a function of whether it was observed being rewarded (Bandura, 1965; Bandura, Ross, & Ross, 1963; Bandura, et al, 1967). Clearly, this type of learning requires complex cognitive processes.

Rescorla (1988) also provides compelling evidence regarding the role played by cognition in basic conditioning processes, arguing that the "information value" of stimuli may be more important than the precise temporal connection between them. Stated simply, stimuli that consistently predict certain events are more likely to leave us believing that they are important. When parents and educators consistently enforce the limits they set, these stated limits gain high information value.

These provocative finding have particular relevance when considering the subject of child maltreatment. A common argument made by proponents of strict behaviorism is that consequences must be provided immediately after an infraction. Fay and Cline contend that a significant portion of abuse in homes (and schools) results from parents trying to provide discipline in the "heat of the moment." Rescorla's work suggests otherwise. As a result, the Love and Logic approach emphasizes:

- When you are too angry to think straight, delay the consequence.
- Effective parents and educators are most concerned with providing appropriate consequences that teach pro-social behavior, than administering quick ones that may or may not achieve this goal.
- The "information value" of a parent or teacher's words is more important than how quickly they provide consequences. Too many adults make rash threats and find that they are unable to follow through on the discipline they promise. Under these circumstances, the attempts to provide immediate consequences actually undermine their disciplinary goals.
- When children observe adults controlling their own behavior by delaying action until they are calm, they have an opportunity to learn these same self-regulation skills.

Festinger's (1957) Theory of Cognitive Dissonance has significantly shaped the Love and Logic theory of change, particularly as it applies to modifying children's attitudes toward academic achievement and positive behavior. According to Festinger, an uncomfortable state of "cognitive dissonance" develops when individuals perform behaviors inconsistent with their beliefs. To relieve this discomfort, a person has two basic options: (1) stop performing the behavior; or (2) change one's beliefs to align with the behavior. Practical implications of this theory present themselves when attribution processes are considered. Attitude change resulting from cognitive dissonance is less likely to occur when individuals are able to attribute the inconsistent behavior to external pressures or temptations. Conversely, beliefs are more likely to align with new behavior when such external sources of justification are absent.

A study by Aronson and Carlsmith (1963) demonstrated these processes at work in an early childhood classroom. Both groups of children were told not to play with a newly introduced toy. One group was warned of significant consequences if they broke the rule. A second group was warned of only mild consequences for breaking this rule. Not surprisingly, the children warned of more significant consequences rated the toy as being far more appealing than those warned of only mild ones. From a theoretical standpoint, dissonance was reduced in the significant consequence group because the children were able to reason, "If I played with the toy knowing that I would be in big trouble, that toy must really be something special! How could I help myself?"

As a result of these and other findings, the Love and Logic theory of change places heavy emphasis on the following:

- Effective parents and educators avoid providing threats and lectures, because doing so provides children with an opportunity to attribute rule breaking and rule following to external variables, rather than new and more positive attitudes.
- Effective parents and educators also rely as little as possible on promising children tangible rewards for desired behavior. While appropriate in certain circumstances, doing so provides an opportunity for young people to attribute

their good behavior to the promised reward rather than a changed mind.

- Behavior and attitude change is primarily achieved by allowing children to learn from modeling, direct instruction, positive feedback on performance, and opportunities to solve the problems they create.

Attributions also have a powerful impact on academic achievement motivation. According to Weiner (1979), high achievers are more likely to attribute their performance to controllable factors, such as their level of effort or perseverance. Low achievers, in contrast, tend to attribute performance to uncontrollable factors, such as luck, the actions of others, or intelligence. A strong body of research has consistently supported these propositions (Diener, C. & Dweck, C.,1978; Dweck & Leggett, 1988; Elliott & Dweck, 1988; Diener & Dweck, 1980, 2000, 2012).

Interestingly, Mueller and Dweck (1998) observed a consistent effect across six studies: Children praised for ability were less likely to persevere when confronted with difficult tasks, displayed less enjoyment of such tasks and actually performed more poorly than those who've received feedback emphasizing effort.

Based on this body of research, the Love and Logic theory of change posits the following:

- The focus must be placed on helping children see the contribution of personal effort and perseverance to achievement.
- Effective parents and educators replace feedback like, "That's great! You are so smart" with "How did you achieve that? Did you work really hard or keep trying?"
- Adults model healthy attributions by thinking out loud around young people, allowing them to overhear statements such as, "This was really challenging for me, but I'm glad that I kept trying."

RELATIONSHIP AND HUMAN NEED THEORIES.

The Love and Logic theory of change was strongly shaped by the clinical experiences of Fay and Cline suggesting that treatment gains and maintenance of such gains suffered when underlying physical and emotional needs were not considered. Converging with this clinical experience is the work of Maslow (1943), Glasser (1969), and Rogers (1957, 1961), suggesting that optimal outcomes are only possible when such needs are met within the context of supportive, accepting relationships. Supporting this early theory is the strong body of research addressed above documenting the supreme importance of positive parent-child and teacher-student relationships. Therefore, the Love and Logic theory of change proposes the following:

- Positive relationships are inherently therapeutic.
- Parents and educators must understand that the effectiveness of all interventions hinges on the quality of the adult-child relationship and the child's social connection with the classroom and family team.
- Children must feel physically and emotionally safe. Otherwise, these needs will take precedence over pro-social behavior and academic motivation.
- Parents and educators must allow children to experience freedom within appropriate developmental limits.
- Effective educators and parents help build self-efficacy by guiding children toward genuine, effort-based success experiences.
- Effective educators and parents have fun while teaching and parenting, and they help children see that learning and behaving can be enjoyable.

Resiliency Theories. Benson, Galbraith, and Espeland (1995) in their study of 270,000 students grades six through twelve, observed a number of "developmental assets" which help children avoid academic failure, emotional problems, criminal behavior, substance abuse, and other negative outcomes. Similar findings have been obtained by others (see Garmezy, 1994; Luthar & Zigler, 1991; Masten & Coatsworth, 1998; Werner & Smith, 1992). Resiliency factors directly addressed by the Love and Logic theory of change are as follows:

- Highly supportive and loving families and schools.
- Parents who establish open communication with their children.
- Positive parent-teacher relationships and parent involvement.
- Positive school climate.
- Appropriate standards for behavior at home and school (i.e., limits).
- Positive school and parental discipline.
- Positive relationships between children and adults other than parents.
- Learning to use empathy with others.
- Decision-making skills.
- Self-esteem.

Current Research Initiative

At this time, ongoing research is being conducted, continuing to examine the effectiveness of the Love and Logic parent and educator training programs using quasi-experimental methods. If you are interested in participating, please contact Dr. Charles Fay at drcfay@loveandlogic.com.

References

Albin, R., Lucyshyn, J., Horner, R., & Flannery, K. (1996). Contextual fit for behavioral support plans. In L. Koegil, R. Koegil, & G. Dunlap (Eds.), *Positive behavioral support: Including people with difficult behaviors in the community* (pp. 81-97). Baltimore, MD: Brookes.

Aronson, E. and Carlsmith, J. (1963) Effects of severity of threat in the devaluation of forbidden behavior, *Journal of Abnormal and Social Psychology*, 66, 584-588.

American Educator (1996). Elements of an effective discipline strategy. *American Educator*, 19, 24-27.

Bandura, A. (1965). Influence of models' reinforcement contingencies on the acquisition of imitative responses. *Journal of Personality and Social Psychology*, 1, 589-595.

Bandura, A. (1977). Self-efficacy: Toward a unifying theory of behavioral change. *Psychological Review*, 84, 191-215.

Bandura, A. (1976). Effecting change through participant modeling principles. In J.D. Krumboltz & C.E. Thorensen (Eds.), *Self-control: Power to the person* (pp. 86 – 110). Pacific Grove, CA: Brooks/Cole.

Bandura, A. (1977). *Social Learning Theory*. Englewood Cliffs, NJ: Prentice-Hall.

Bandura, A., Grusec, J., & Menlove, F. (1967). Vicarious extinction of avoidance behavior. *Journal of Personality and Social Psychology*, 5, 16-23.

Bandura, A. & Jeffery, R. (1973). Role of symbolic coding and rehearsal processes in observational learning. *Journal of Personality and Social Psychology*, 26, 122-130.

Bandura, A., Barbaranelli, C., Caprara, G. V., & Pastorelli, C. (1996). Multifaceted impact of self-efficacy beliefs on academic functioning. *Child Development*, 67, 1206–1222.

Bandura, A., Ross, D., & Ross, S. (1961). Transmission of aggression through imitation of aggressive models. *Journal of Abnormal and Social Psychology*, 63, 575-582.

Bandura, A., Ross, D., & Ross, S. (1963). Vicarious reinforcement and imitative learning. *Journal of Personality and Social Psychology*, 67, 601-607.

Baumrind, D. (1991). The influence of parenting style on adolescent competence and substance use. *Journal of Early Adolescence*, 11, 56–95.

Baumrind, D. (1996). The discipline controversy revisited. *Family Relations*, 45, 405 – 414.

Barber, B. & Olsen, J. (1997). Socialization in context: Connection, regulation, and autonomy in the family, school, and neighborhood, and with peers. *Journal of Adolescent Research*, 12, 287–315.

Barnoski, R. (2004). *Outcome evaluation of Washington State's research-based programs for juvenile offenders*. Olympia, WA: Washington State Institute for Public Policy.

Benson, P. (2006). *All kids are our kids: What communities must do to raise caring and responsible children and adolescents*. San Francisco: Jossey Bass.

Benson, P., Espeland, P., & Galbraith, J. (1994). *What kids need to succeed*. Minneapolis: Free Spirit.

Benson, P., Leffert, N., Scales, P., & Blyth, D. (1998). Beyond the "village" rhetoric: Creating healthy communities for children and adolescents. *Applied Developmental Science*, 2, 138–159.

Benson, P., Galbraith, J., & Espeland, P. (1995). *What kids need to succeed: Proven, practical ways to raise good kids*. Minneapolis, MN: Free Spirit Publishing.

Bond, R., & Saunders, P. (1999). Routes of success: Influences on the occupational attainment of young British males. *British Journal of Sociology*, 50, 217–249.

Bradley, R. & Corwyn, R. (2007). Externalizing problems in fifth grade: Relations with productive activity, maternal sensitivity, and harsh parenting from infancy through middle childhood. *Developmental Psychology*, 43, 1390–1401.

Brophy, J. (1983). Research on the self-fulfilling prophecy and teacher expectations. *Journal of Educational Psychology*, 75, 631-661.

Bromfield, C. (2006). PGCE secondary trainee teachers & effective behavior management: An evaluation and commentary. *Support for Learning*, 21, 188-193.

Bronfenbrenner, U. (1979). *The ecology of human development*. Cambridge, MA: Harvard University Press.

Bronfenbrenner, U. & Morris, P. (2006). *The bioecological model of human development*. Wiley Online Library.

Browne, K. (2013). Challenging behavior in secondary school students: Classroom strategies for increasing positive behavior. *New Zealand Journal of Teachers' Work*, 125-147.

Carnine, D. (1997). Bridging the research-to-practice gap. *Exceptional Children*, 63, 513-521.

Casanova, P., García-Linares, M., de la Torre, M., & de la Villa Carpio, M. (2005). Influence of family and socio-demographic variables on students with low academic achievement. *Educational Psychology*, 25, 423–435.

Cerdorian, K. (2006). The relationship between parenting style, parenting stress, and a parenting intervention. Unpublished doctoral dissertation. The University of Northern Colorado.

Chiu, L. & Tulley, M. (1997). Student preferences of teacher discipline styles. *Journal of Instructional Psychology*, 24, 168-175.

Clark, R., Dogan, R., & Akbar, N. (2003). Youth and parental correlates of externalizing symptoms, adaptive functioning, and academic performance: An exploratory study in preadolescent Blacks. *Journal of Black Psychology*, 29, 210–229.

Cline, F. & Fay, J. (1990). *Parenting with love and logic*. Colorado Springs, CO: Pinon Press.

Cline, F. & Fay, J. (1993). *Parenting teens with love and logic*. Colorado Springs, CO: Pinon Press.

Clunies-Ross, P., Little, E., & Kienhuis, M. (2008). Self-reported and actual use of proactive and reactive classroom management strategies and their relationship with teacher stress and student behaviour. *Educational Psychology*, 28, 693–710.

Cormier, W. & Cormier, S. (1991). *Interviewing skills for helpers: Fundamental skills and cognitive behavioral interventions*. Pacific Grove, CA: Brooks/Cole.

Costello, E. J., Keeler, G. P., & Angold, A. (2001). Poverty, race/ethnicity, and psychiatric disorder: A study of rural children. *American Journal of Public Health*, 91, 1494–1498.

Cotton, K. (1990). *School Improvement Series. Close up #9: Schoolwide and classroom discipline*. Portland, OR: Northwest Regional Education Laboratory.

Crowe, C. (2013). A longitudinal investigation of parent educational involvement and student achievement: Disentangling parent socialization and child evocative effects across development. *Journal of Educational Research & Policy Studies*, 13, 1-32.

Daniels, M. (2009). The three Fs of classroom management. *AASA Journal of Scholarship and Practice*, 6, 18-24.

de Boer, H., Bosker, R., & van der Werf, M. (2010). Sustainability of teacher expectation bias effects on long-term student performance. *Journal of Educational Psychology*, 102, 168–179.

Diener, C. & Dweck, C. (1978). An analysis of learned helplessness: Continuous changes in performance, strategy, and achievement cognitions following failure. *Journal of Personality and Social Psychology*, 36, 451-462.

Diener, C. I. & Dweck, C. S. (1980). An analysis of learned helplessness: II. The processing of success. *Journal of Personality and Social Psychology*, 39, 940–952.

Dishion, T. J. (1990). Peer context of troublesome behavior in children and adolescents. In P. Leone (Ed.), *Understanding Troubled and Troublesome Youth*. Beverly Hill: Sage.

Doren, B., Gau, J., & Lindstrom, M. (2012). The relationship between parent expectations and postschool outcomes of adolescents with disabilities. *Council for Exceptional Children*, 79, 7-23.

Dweck, C. (2000). *Self-theories: Their role in motivation, personality, and development*. Philadelphia, PA: Psychology Press.

Dweck, C. (2012). Implicit theories. In P. A. M. Van Lange, A. W. Kruglanski, & E. T. Higgins (Eds.), *Handbook of theories of social psychology*, 2, 43–61. Thousand Oaks, CA: Sage.

Dweck, C. S. & Leggett, E. L. (1988). A social-cognitive approach to motivation and personality. *Psychological Review*, 95, 256–273.

D'Zurilla, T. (1986). *Problem-solving therapy: A social competence approach to clinical intervention*. New York: Springer.

Eccles, J., Wigfield, A., & Schiefele, U. (1998). Motivation to succeed. In W. Damon (Series Ed.) & N. Eisenberg (Vol. Ed.), *Handbook of Child Development: Vol. 3, Social Emotional and Personality Development* (5th ed. pp. 1017–1095). New York: Wiley.

Egger, H. & Angold, A. (2006). Common emotional and behavioral disorders in preschool children: Presentation, nosology, and epidemiology. *Journal of Child Psychology and Psychiatry*, 47, 313–337.

Eisenberg, N., & Murphy, B. (1995). Parenting and children's moral development. In M. H. Bornstein (Ed.), *Handbook of Parenting*, 4, 227–257). Mahwah: Erlbaum.

Elam, S., Rose, L., & Gallup, A. (1996). Twenty-eighth annual Phi Delta Kappa/Gallup poll of the public's attitudes toward the public schools. *Phi Delta Kappan*, 78, 41-59.

Elliott, E. & Dweck, C. (1988). Goals: An approach to motivation and achievement. *Journal of Personality and Social Psychology*, 54, 5-12.

Englund, M., Luckner, A., Whaley, G., & Egeland, B. (2004). Children's achievement in early elementary school: Longitudinal effects of parental involvement, expectations, and quality of assistance. *Journal of Educational Psychology*, 96, 723–730.

Emmer, E. & Evertson, C. (1981). Synthesis of research on classroom management. *Educational Leadership*, 38, 342-347.

Emmer, E., Evertson, C., & Anderson, L. (1980). Effective classroom management at the beginning of the school year. *Elementary School Journal*, 80, 219-231.

Fan, X. & Chen, M. (2001). Parental involvement and students' academic achievement: A metaanalysis. *Educational Psychology Review*, 13, 1–22.

Fay, C. (2007). Effects of the 9 Essential Skills for the Love and Logic Classroom training program on teachers' perceptions of their students' behavior and their own teaching competence: A preliminary investigation. Unpublished outcome data. The Love and Logic Institute: Golden, Colorado.

Fay, C. (2012). Effects of the Becoming a Love and Logic Parent Training Program on parents' perceptions of their children's behavior and their own parenting stress. Unpublished outcome data. The Love and Logic Institute: Golden, Colorado.

Fay, J. & Fay, C. (2012) 9 Essential Skills for the Love and Logic Classroom. Golden, Colorado: The Love and Logic Institute, Inc.

Fay, J & Fay, C. (2012) Parenting the Love and Logic Way. Golden, Colorado: The Love and Logic Institute, Inc.

Fay, J. & Cline, F. (1997). *Discipline with love and logic teacher training course*. Golden, CO: The Love and Logic Press.

Fay, J. & Funk, D. (1995). *Teaching with love and logic*. Golden, CO: The Love and Logic Press.

Ferster, C.B. & Skinner, B.F. (1957). *Schedules of Reinforcement*. New York: Appleton-Century-Crofts.

Festinger, L. (1957) *A Theory of Cognitive Dissonance*, Stanford, CA: Stanford University Press.

Fideler, E. & Haselkorn, D. (1999). *Learning the ropes: Urban Teacher Induction Programs and Practices in the United States*. Belmont, MA: Recruiting New Teachers.

Fields, B. (2000). School discipline: Is there a crisis in our schools? *Australian Journal of Social Issues*, 35, 73.

Finn, J. (1989). Withdrawing from school. *Review of Educational Research*, 59, 117-142.

Flouril E. & Hawkes, D. (2008). Ambitious mothers – successful daughters: Mothers' early expectations for children's education and children's earnings and sense of control in adult life. *British Journal of Educational Psychology*, 78, 411–433.

Foshee, V. & Bauman, K. (1994). Parental attachment and adolescent cigarette smoking initiation. *Journal of Adolescent Research*, 9, 88–104.

Foster, S., Prinz, R., & O'Leary, K. (1983). Impact of problem-solving communication training and generalization procedures on family conflict. *Child and Family Behavior Therapy*, 5, 1–23.

Frier, R. (2003). Ridgeview Global Studies Academy Discipline Report – 2000-01, 2001-02, and 2002-03. Unpublished School Data. Ridgeview Global Studies Academy, Davenport, FL.

Ganzach, Y. (2000). Parents' education, cognitive ability, educational expectations and educational attainment: Interactive effects. *British Journal of Educational Psychology*, 70, 419–441.

Garrett, T. (2014). Classroom management: A world of misconceptions. *Teaching & Learning*, 28, 36-43.

Garmezy, N. (1994). Reflections and commentary on risk, resilience, and development. In R.J. Haggerty, L. Sherrod, N. Garmezy, & M. Rutter (Eds.), *Stress, Risk, and Resilience in Children and Adolescents: Processes, Mechanisms, and Interventions*. New York: Cambridge University Press.

Glasser, W. (1969). *Schools without failure*. New York: Harper & Row.

Glick, B. & Gibbs, J. (2011). *Aggression replacement training, third edition*. Champaign, IL: Research Press.

Good, T. & Nichols, L. (2001). Expectancy Effects in the Classroom: A Special Focus on Improving the Reading Performance of Minority Students in First-Grade Classrooms. *Educational Psychologist*, 36, 113–126.

Goyette, K. & Xie, Y. (1999). Educational expectations of Asian American youths: Determinants and ethnic differences. *Sociology of Education*, 72, 22–36.

Graf, F., Grumm, M., Hein, S., & Fingerle, M. (2014). Improving Parental Competencies: Subjectively Perceived Usefulness of a Parent Training Matters. *Journal of Child and Family Studies*, 23, 20–28.

Gresham, F., Mai Bao, V., & Cook, C. (2006). Social skills training for teaching replacement behaviors: Remediating acquisition deficits in at-risk students. *Behavioral Disorders*, 31 (4), 363–377.

Grusec, J. & Goodnow, J. (1994). Impact of parental discipline method on the child's internalization of values: A reconceptualization of current of view. *Developmental Psychology*, 30, 4–19.

Hamre, B. & Pianta, R. (2001). Early teacher-child relationships and the trajectory of children's school outcomes through eighth grade. *Child Development*, 72, 625-638.

Hamre, B. & Pianta, R. (2005). Can instructional and emotional support in the first-grade classroom make a difference for children at risk of school failure? *Child Development*, 76, 949-967.

Harris, M. & Rosenthal, R. (1985). Mediation of interpersonal expectancy effects: 31 metaanalyses, *Psychological Bulletin*, 97, 363-386.

Hayek, M. (2001). *Effects of Parent Training With Love and Logic at Navigator School*. Unpublished research conducted in collaboration with Wayne State University.

Hazel, N., Oppenheimer, C., & Technow, J. (2014). Relationship quality buffers against the effect of peer stressors on depressive symptoms from middle childhood to adolescence. *Developmental Psychology*, 50, 2115–2123.

Heaven, P. & Newbury, K. (2004). Relationships between adolescent and parental characteristics and adolescents' attitudes to school and self-rated academic performance. *Australian Journal of Psychology*, 56, 173–180.

Huebner, A. & Betts, S. (2002). Exploring the utility of social bond theory for youth development. *Youth & Society*, 34, 123–145.

Johnson, M. (2014). The efficacy of using enforceable statements as a high school classroom management technique. Unpublished doctoral dissertation. Jones International University.

Johnson, V., Cowan, P., & Cowan, C. (1999). Children's classroom behavior: The unique contribution of family organization. *Journal of Family Psychology*, 13, 355–371.

Jordan Irvine, J. (2002). African American teachers' culturally specific pedagogy: The collective stories. In J. Jordan Irvine (Ed.), *In search of wholeness: African American Teachers and Their Culturally Specific Classroom Practices*. New York: Palgrave.

Juang, L. & Silbereisen, R. (2002). The relationship between adolescent academic capability beliefs, parenting and school grades. *Journal of Adolescence*, 25, 3–18.

Karofsky, P., Zeng, L., & Kosorok, M. (2000). Relationship between adolescent-parental communication and initiation of first intercourse by adolescents. *Journal of Adolescent Health*, 28, 41–45.

Kazdin, A. (1981). Acceptability of child treatment techniques: The influence of treatment efficacy and adverse side effects. *Behavior Therapy*, 12, 453-506.

Kerr, M. & Bowen, M. (1988). *Family Evaluation: An approach based on Bowen Theory* New York: W. W. Norton & Company, Inc.

Kern, L. & Manz, P. (2004). A look at current validity issues of schoolwide behavior support. *Behavioral Disorders*, 30, 47-59.

Kounin, J. (1970). *Discipline and Group Management in the Classroom*. New York: Hold, Rinehart and Winston.

Kramer-Schlosser, L. (1992). Teacher distance and student disengagement: Schools live on the margin. *Journal of Teacher Education*, 43, 128-140.

Kwon, J., Chung, C., & Lee, J. (2009). The effects of escape from self and interpersonal relationship on the pathological use of internet games. *Community Mental Health Journal*, 47, 112-121

La Rosa, S., Kiernan, J., Shaw-Reeves, R., Baker, R., Wolf-Branigan, M., & Hayek, M. (2001). *Collaborative action research using Discipline with Love and Logic*. Unpublished research conducted in collaboration between Wayne State University and Navigator School.

Larson, R., Eccles, J., & Gootman, J. (2004). Features of positive developmental settings. *The Prevention Researcher*, 11, 8–12.

Laundra, K., Kiger, G., & Bahr, S. (2002). A social development model of serious delinquency: Examining gender differences. *Journal of Primary Prevention*, 22, 389–407.

Lee, S., Hong, S., & Park, J. (2005). The study of the personal and social influence on internet addiction among adolescents. *The Korean Journal of Educational Psychology*, 19, 1179-1197.

Lewis, T., Colvin, G., & Sugai, G. (2000). The effects of pre-correction and active supervision on the recess behavior of elementary students. *Education and Treatment of Children*, 2, 109-121.

Lewis, T., Sugai, G., & Colvin, G. (1998). Reducing problem behavior through a schoolwide system of effective behavioral support: Investigation of a schoolwide social skills training program and contextual interventions. *School Psychology Review*, 27, 446-459.

Lundeen, C. (2002). *The study of beginning teachers' perceived problems with classroom management and adult relationships throughout the first year of teaching*. Unpublished doctoral dissertation, University of North Carolina, Chapel Hill.

Luthar, S. & Zigler, E. (1991). Vulnerability and competence: A review of research on resilience in childhood. *American Journal of Orthopsychiatry*, 61, 6-22.

Maag, J. (2005). Social skills training for youth with emotional and behavioral disorders and learning disabilities: Problems, conclusions, and suggestions. *Exceptionality*, 13, 155–172.

Maccoby, E. & Martin, J. (1983). Socialization in the context of the family: Parent-child interaction. In E. M. Hetherington (Ed.), *Handbook of child psychology: Socialization, Personality, and Social Development*, 4, 1–101. New York: Wiley.

Marzano, R., Marzano, J., & Pickering, D. (2003). *Classroom Management That Works: Research-Based Strategies for Every Teacher*. Alexandria, VA: ASCD.

Maslow, A. (1943). A theory of human motivation, *Psychological Review*, 50, 370-396.

Mayer, G. & Sulzer-Azaroff, B. (1991). Interventions for vandalism. In G. Stoner, M. Shinn, & H. Walker (Eds.), *Interventions for Achievement and Behavior Problems*. Washington, DC: National Association of School Psychologists.

McKenna, J. (1997) *Effects of Systematic Noticing on a Withdrawn Student's Self-Concept*. Unpublished master's degree thesis.

McMahon, R. & Estes. A. (1997). Conduct problems. In E. J. Mash & L. G. Terdal (Eds.), *Assessment of Childhood Disorders* (3rd ed.). New York: Guilford Press.

Minuchin, P. (1985). Families and individual development: Provocations from the Field of Family Therapy. *Child Development*, 56, 289-302.

Miramontes, N., Marchant, M., Allen, M., & Fischer, L. (2011). Social Validity of a Positive Behavior Interventions and Support Model. *Education and Treatment of Children*, 34, 445-469.

Mistry, R., White, E., Benner, A., & Huynh, V. (2009). A longitudinal study of the simultaneous influence of mothers' and teachers' educational expectations on low-income youth's academic achievement. *Journal of Youth and Adolescence*, 38, 826–838.

Mitchell, C. (2009). *Teaching Prosocial Skills to Antisocial Youth. Aggregate Evaluation Dashboard Report*. Sacramento, CA: California Institute for Mental Health.

Morganett, L. (1991). Good teacher-student relationships: A key element in classroom motivation and management. *Education*, 112, 260-264.

Mueller, C. & Dweck, C. (1998). Praise for intelligence can undermine children's motivation and performance. *Journal of Personality and Social Psychology*, 75,   33-52.

Murray, C. & Malmgren, K. (2005). Implementing a teacher-student relationship program in a high-poverty urban school: Effects on social, emotional, and academic adjustment and lessons learned. *Journal of School Psychology*, 43, 137-152.

National Institute of Mental Health (2002). *Blueprint for Change: Research on Child and Adolescent Mental Health*. Washington, DC: Department of Health and Human Services.

Nelson, J., Colvin, G., & Smith, D. (1996). The effects of setting clear standards on students' social behavior in common areas of the school. *The Journal of At-Risk Issues*, 3, 10-19.

Oswald, K., Safran, S., & Johanson. (2005). Preventing Trouble: Making Schools Safer Places Using Positive Behavior Supports. *Education and Treatment of Children*, 28, 265-278.

Patterson, G., Reid, J., & Dishion, T. (1992). *Antisocial Boys: Vol 4. A Social Interactional Approach*. Eugene: Castalia.

Pavlov, I. (1927). *Conditioned Reflexes: An Investigation of the Physiological Activity of the Cerebral Cortex.* Translated and Edited by G. V. Anrep. London: Oxford University Press.

Pomerantz, E., Ng, F., & Wang, Q. (2006). Mothers' mastery-oriented involvement in children's homework: Implications for the well-being of children with negative perceptions of competence. *Journal of Educational Psychology*, 98, 99–111.

Pomerantz, E. & Wei, D. (2006). Effects of mothers' perceptions of children's competence: The moderating role of mothers' theories of competence. *Developmental Psychology*, 42, 950–961.

Public Health Service, U. S. (2000). *Report of the Surgeon General's Conference on Children's Mental Health: A National Agenda.* Washington, DC: U.S. Government Printing Office.

Ream, G. & Savin-Williams, R. (2005). Reciprocal associations between adolescent sexual activity and quality of youth-parent interactions. *Journal of Family Psychology*, 19, 171–179.

Regalado, M. & Halfon, N. (2002). *Primary Care Services: Promoting Optimal Child Development from Birth to Three Years.* The Commonwealth Fund.

Rescorla, R. (1988). Pavlovian conditioning: It's not what you think it is. *American Psychologist*, 43, 151-160.

Richaud, M., Mesurado, B., & Lemos, V. (2013). Links between perception of parental actions and prosocial behavior in early adolescence. *Journal of Child and Family Studies*, 22, 637–646.

Robertson, D. & Reynolds, A. (2010). Family profiles and educational attainment. *Children and Youth Services Review*, 32, 1077–1085.

Rogers, C. (1957). The necessary and sufficient conditions of therapeutic personality change. *Journal of Consulting Psychology*, 21, 95–103.

Rogers, C. (1961). *On Becoming a Person.* Boston: Houghton Mifflin.

Roorda, D., Koomen, H., Spilt, J., & Oort, F. (2011). The influence of affective teacher-student relationships on students' school engagement and achievement. *Review of Educational Research*, 81, 493-529.

Rosenthal, R. & Jacobson, L. (1968). *Pygmalion in the Classroom: Teacher Expectation and Pupils' Intellectual Development*. New York: Holt.

Rosenthal, R. (1985). From unconscious experimenter bias to teacher expectancy effects. In J. Dusek, V. Hall, & W. Meyer (Eds.), *Teacher Expectancies*. Hillsdale, NJ: Lawrence Erlbaum Associates, Inc.

Sandefur, G., Meier, A., & Campbell, M. (2006). Family resources, social capital, and college attendance. *Social Science Research*, 35, 525–553.

Salzinger, S. (1992). The role of social networks in adaptation throughout the life cycle. In M. S. Gibbs, J. R. Lachenmeyer, & J. S. Sigal (Eds.), *Community Psychology and Mental Health*. New York, NY: Gardner Press.

Schwartz, I. & Baer, D.(1991). Social validity assessments: Is current practice state of the art? *Journal of Applied Behavior Analysis*, 24, 186-212.

Seeley, J., Stice, E., & Rohde, P. (2009). Screening for depression prevention: Identifying adolescent girls at high risk for future depression. *Journal of Abnormal Psychology*, 118, 161–170.

Shapiro, C., Prinz, R., & Sanders, M. (2008). Population-Wide Parenting Intervention Training: Initial Feasibility. *Journal of Child and Family Studies*, 17, 457–466.

Sheeber, L., Hops, H., Alpert, A., Davis, B., & Andrews, J. (1997). Family support and conflict: Prospective relations to adolescent depression. *Journal of Abnormal Child Psychology*, 25, 333–344.

Schlechty (1990). *Schools for the 21st Century*. San Francisco: Josey-Bass.

Schroeder, V. & Kelley, M. (2009). Associations between family environment, parenting practices, and executive functioning of children with and without ADHD. *Journal of Child and Family Studies*, 18, 227–235

Skinner, B.F. (1974). *About Behaviorism*. New York: Alfred A. Knopf.

Skinner, B.F (1953). *Science and Human Behavior*. New York: Macmillan

Smith, T. E. (1981). Adolescent agreement with perceived maternal and paternal educational goals. *Journal of Marriage and the Family*, 43, 85–93.

Spivak, G. & Sure, M. (1974). *The Problem-Solving Approach to Adjustment*. San Francisco, CA: Jossey-Bass.

Spoth, R. & Redmond, C. (1995). Parent motivation to enroll in parenting skills programs: A model of family context and health belief predictors. *Journal of Family Psychology*, 9, 294–310.

Stice, E., Ragan, J., & Randall, P. (2004). Prospective relations between social support and depression: Differential direction of effects for parent and peer support. *Journal of Abnormal Psychology*, 113, 155–159.

Thorndike, E. (1911). *Animal Intelligence: Experimental Studies*. New York: MacMillan.

Todd, A., Horner, R., Anderson, K., & Spriggs, M. (2002). Teaching recess: Low-cost efforts producing effective results. *Journal of Positive Behavior Interventions*, 4, 46-52.

Ullucci, K. (2009). "This has to be family": Humanizing classroom management in urban schools. *Journal of Classroom Interaction*, 44, 13-28.

Walker, H. (1998). First steps to prevent antisocial behavior. *Teaching Exceptional Children*, 30, 16–9.

Walker, H., Colvin, G., & Ramsey, E. (1995). Antisocial Behavior in School: Strategies and Best Practices. Pacific Grove: Brooks/Cole Publishing Company.

Walker, H., Ramsey, E., & Gresham, F. (2004). *Antisocial Behavior in School: Evidence-Based Practices* (2nd ed.). Belmont, CA: Wadsworth/Thompson.

Watson, J. & Rayner, R. (1920). Conditioned emotional reactions. *Journal of Experimental Psychology*, 3(1), 1-14.

Weiner, B. (1979). A theory of motivation for some classroom experiences. *Journal of Educational Psychology*, 71, 3-25.

Weinstein, R., Marshall, H., Brattesani, K., & Middlestadt, S. (1982). Student perceptions of differential teacher treatment in open and traditional classrooms. *Journal of Educational Psychology*, 75, 678-692.

Weinstein, R. & Middlestadt, S. (1979). Student perceptions of teacher interactions with male high and low achievers. *Journal of Educational Psychology*, 71, 421-431.

Wigfield, A. & Eccles, J. (2002). The development of competence beliefs, expectancies for success, and achievement values from childhood through adolescence. In G. Phye (Ed.), *Development of Achievement Motivation*. San Diego: Academic Press.

Witt, J. & Elliott, S. (1985). *Acceptability of classroom management strategies*. In T.R. Kratochwill (Ed.), Advances in School Psychology (Vol. 4). Hillsdale, HJ: Lawrence Erlbaum.

Wolf, M. (1978). Social validity: The case for subjective measurement or how applied behavior analysis is finding its heart. *Journal of Applied Behavior Analysis*, 11, 203-214.

Wu, J., Hughes, & Kwok, O. (2010). Teacher-student relationship quality type in elementary grades: Effects on trajectories for achievement and engagement. *Journal of School Psychology*, 48, 357-387.

Wubbels, T., Brekelmans, M., van Tartwijk, J., Admiral, W. (1999). Interpersonal relationships between teachers and students in the classroom. In H. C. Waxman & H.J. Walberg (Eds.), *New Directions for Teaching Practice and Research*, 151-170. Berkeley, CA: McCutchan.

Zhang, Y., Haddad, E., Torres, B., & Chuansheng, C. (2011). The Reciprocal Relationships Among Parents' Expectations, Adolescents' Expectations, and Adolescents' Achievement: A Two-Wave Longitudinal Analysis of the NELS Data. *Journal of Youth and Adolescence*, 40, 479–489.

Index